Penguin Masterstudies

King Lear

Kenneth Muir is Professor Emeritus in English Literature at the University of Liverpool. He has an international reputation as a Shakespeare scholar and is the editor of the Arden edition of *King Lear*. He was editor of *Shakespeare Survey* between 1965 and 1980, and continued as Chairman of the International Shakespeare Association. He has prepared numerous critical editions of the works of major poets and dramatists as well as being the author of many critical works, including *Shakespeare's Tragic Sequence*. He is known, in addition, as an amateur actor, producer and translator.

Penguin Masterstudies
Advisory Editors:
Stephen Coote and Bryan Loughrey

William Shakespeare

King Lear

Kenneth Muir

Penguin Books

Penguin Books Ltd, 27 Wrights Lane, London W8 5TZ (Publishing and Editorial)
and Harmondsworth, Middlesex, England (Distribution and Warehouse)
Viking Penguin Inc., 40 West 23rd Street, New York, New York 10010, USA
Penguin Books Australia Ltd, Ringwood, Victoria, Australia
Penguin Books Canada Ltd, 2801 John Street, Markham, Ontario, Canada L3R 1B4
Penguin Books (NZ) Ltd, 182–190 Wairau Road, Auckland 10, New Zealand

First published 1986
Reprinted 1986, 1987

Made and printed in Great Britain by
Richard Clay Ltd, Bungay, Suffolk

Contents

Introduction

In spite of Charles Lamb's notorious pronouncement that Shakespeare's tragedies, and especially *King Lear*, could not be acted,[1] the proper place for the play is not the study or the classroom, but the theatre. Lamb, indeed, had been irritated by the fact that Garrick's admirers had placed him beside Shakespeare; but it is not always realized that Lamb had never seen Shakespeare's play performed but only Nahum Tate's adaptation of it, which held the stage for a century and a half and was banished only after Lamb's death. Tate omitted the Fool; and at the end Lear is restored to the throne and Cordelia is married to Edgar, whom she had loved all along.

There is, however, an element of truth in Lamb's argument. Many productions, it must be admitted, are disappointing:

> So to see Lear acted – to see an old man tottering about the stage with a walking-stick, turned out of doors by his daughters in a rainy night, has nothing in it but what is painful and disgusting. We want to take him into shelter and relieve him. That is all the feeling which the acting of Lear ever produced in me. But the Lear of Shakespeare cannot be acted. The contemptible machinery by which they mimic the storm which he goes out in, is not more inadequate to represent the horrors of the real elements, than any actor can be to represent Lear ... The greatness of Lear is not in corporal dimension, but in intellectual: the explosions of his passion are terrible as a volcano; they are storms turning up and disclosing to the bottom that sea, his mind, with all its vast riches.

In the Commentary on Act III (p. 76), we shall see that it is possible to perform the storm-scenes without betraying the poetic conception. The 'contemptible machinery' of which Lamb speaks has been transformed by the invention of electric light and by the revolution in staging brought about by the scrapping of representational scenery. There are still a few directors who vulgarize the play by attempting to be naturalistic or too clever by half, but anyone who has seen Gielgud, Olivier, Redgrave and three or four other Lears will know that a stage performance can be profoundly satisfying, and need not send us away feeling that the secret performance in our mind was more in tune with Shakespeare's conception of the play.

It is necessary to read the play to understand it fully; but it is equally necessary to see the play performed, if possible in a live performance in the theatre. If none is immediately available, one has to make do with television or screen performances.[2] We shall therefore be considering *King Lear* primarily as a stage play, that is, as a poetic drama written for the Elizabethan stage; but such a consideration involves those aspects of the play which are too often regarded as literary rather than theatrical. Poetry, imagery, character, symbolism and theme cannot be divorced from their practical function in the theatre. Even A. C. Bradley, who used to be written off as anti-theatrical, declared[3] that he was writing of the characters as though he were a director, instructing his actors on how all the parts should be played. Nor was he indifferent to the poetic atmosphere of the plays, and how this was created.

The second half of this book is a scene-by-scene commentary, geared to the New Penguin Shakespeare edition of G. K. Hunter. In the first half of the book we shall be considering the construction of the play, its characters, themes and images, as a basis for interpretation.

The Making of the Play

We cannot be certain about the genesis of *King Lear* any more than we can of poems by Wordsworth or Keats, whose lives and letters are known in some detail; but we can make informed guesses about the various pressures brought to bear on a dramatist in the early years of the seventeenth century, in particular on a poetic dramatist who was both an actor and one of the chief shareholders in the king's players. Shakespeare was writing for a repertory company with a limited number of actors: he could not, it seems, write a play with as many as six female parts. The leading actor, Richard Burbage, who had been outstandingly successful as Hamlet and Othello, would expect another great part; and Shakespeare, who knew how much the success of his plays depended on the actors, and whose genius matured alongside the increasing subtlety of the techniques of the actors at his disposal, would be anxious to oblige. Another actor in the company, Robert Armin, a goldsmith turned professional, who had played three very different kinds of Fool (Touchstone, Feste and the gloomy Lavache), obviously had to be provided with a suitable part: Lear's Fool was the opportunity he needed.

To be the king's men was an honour which carried with it certain responsibilities and certain anxieties. They would be expected to perform at court when required, and the choice of play was designed to satisfy the royal tastes. James I was a learned man and he fancied himself as a poet. When writing *Othello*, Shakespeare took note of the king's poem on the battle of Lepanto – the battle which saved Europe from the Turks; and soon after, or just before, writing *King Lear*, Shakespeare chose a subject after James's heart. *Macbeth* was concerned with witchcraft, on which James had written a book, with his reputed ancestor, Banquo, and with the Gunpowder Plot, in which – not without reason – he was personally interested.

King Lear was less obviously a play for royal consumption; but the dangers of a divided kingdom was the theme of James's speeches on the desirability of uniting England and Scotland. The earliest English five-act tragedy, written and performed by amateurs two years before Shakespeare's birth, Norton and Sackville's *Gorboduc*, was designed to warn Elizabeth I that if she did not marry and produce an heir, there was a danger of a disputed succession and civil war. The Chorus expressed the moral in plain terms:

And this great king, that doth divide his land ...
And yields the reign into his children's hand,
From blissful state of joy and great renown,
A mirror shall become to princes all,
To learn to shun the cause of such a fall.

There is no doubt that Shakespeare had read *Gorboduc*;[1] and he would know from *The Faerie Queene*'s summary of the reigns of early British kings, and from Holinshed's *Chronicles*, one of the sources of the history plays, that Gorboduc reigned not long after Leir. It is possible, then, that the Leir story suggested itself as a play on the dangers of a divided kingdom. Yet the moral was ambiguous. The dangers were not due to the division of the kingdom as such, but rather to the characters of two of the king's daughters (see p. 54). Kent and Gloucester express surprise that Albany and Cornwall receive equal shares, but they do not disapprove of the plan of dividing the kingdom. Lear's motive – to avoid future strife – was perfectly sensible. If he had died, or become incapable, without arranging the succession, there would certainly have been serious trouble.

Shakespeare, and doubtless some of his audience, would have memories of the old play of *King Leir*, either from seeing it performed or from reading the printed text. His most successful tragedy so far had been a rewriting of the old *Hamlet*; and it would have been natural for him to have considered whether any other earlier play could be transmuted into a masterpiece.

It would, of course, be absurd to pretend that the pressures exerted by court and theatre could in themselves explain the writing of *King Lear*. More important were Shakespeare's development as a poet, and his own inner compulsions. In spite of the fact that audiences generally preferred comedies to tragedies – although *The Spanish Tragedy* and *Hamlet* were exceptionally popular – it was believed by critics that tragedy was the highest kind of drama. With the production of *Julius Caesar*, Shakespeare had emerged as the greatest tragic writer since Sophocles, greater by far than the much-admired Seneca, whose plays, being in Latin, were more accessible to most Elizabethans than those of the Greek poets. Shakespeare in 1605 was at the height of his powers and tragedy was the genre in which he could best display them.

It is probable, too, that he had come to have an increasingly tragic view of life, not because (as Wordsworth put it) poets in their youth 'begin in gladness,/But thereof come in the end despondency and madness', but because of 'the thousand natural shocks/That flesh is heir to', mentioned by Hamlet; or because of his realization, expressed by a minor character in *All's Well That Ends Well*, that 'the web of our life is of a mingled yarn, good and ill together'; or because he was acutely aware, as Keats was on 3 May 1818, 'that the world is full of Misery and Heartbreak, Pain, Sickness and oppression'.

The Lear story existed in dozens of different versions. Some of them (for example, Camden's) were concerned merely with the love-test applied by the king to his three daughters. Other versions (for instance, those of Geoffrey of Monmouth, Spenser, Holinshed, Higgins and Warner) provided a sequel in which Cordelia, after the restoration and death of Lear, was deposed by her nephews and committed suicide in prison. We know from verbal echoes in the text of the play that Shakespeare was acquainted with at least three of these; but the version from which he borrowed most was the old play of *King Leir*, published in 1605, although Shakespeare may have known it before that date.

King Leir has a happy ending, with no premonition of the tragic sequel. After the king has been maltreated by two of his daughters, he is succoured by Cordella and her husband. There is a faithful servant, Perillus, who has some resemblance to Kent, but he is not banished; and Cordella is accompanied by a clownish character called Mumford (see p. 14). The French invasion is successful and Leir is restored to the throne. Shakespeare knew that the play sentimentalized the story by ignoring the tragic sequel. Apart from that, he knew that the Christian setting was anachronistic, since Leir's reign preceded the birth of Christ by many years. What gods were worshipped in Britain in Leir's time – Jupiter, Mars, Mercury, Apollo, and so on – Shakespeare knew from the misleading account by William Harrison prefixed to Holinshed's *Chronicles*. But it was not simply his wish to avoid anachronism – a matter which worried his commentators more than Shakespeare himself – that made him alter the Christian setting of *King Leir*. *Hamlet* and *Othello* are explicitly Christian, and Macbeth confesses that he has sold his soul to the common enemy of man, the devil. Some writers have argued that since the wicked go to hell and the righteous to heaven, a providential and happy ending is inevitable, and a Christian tragedy is therefore impossible. Shakespeare did not share this view; but he may have wished to write a more absolute tragedy, with no assurance that its outcome would be alleviated after death by divine rewards and punishments (see p. 43). A pagan setting, moreover, gave him much greater freedom. He could present ticklish theological issues, in particular the question of providence, without falling foul of the strict Jacobean censorship.

The Leir story may have been particularly attractive to Shakespeare because its central theme was ingratitude, a subject with which he had been obsessed for a number of years. He declared that it bit keener than the winter wind, that it was more lethal than the arms of traitors, that it was worse than any vice, driving Timon into madness and despair.[2] Ingratitude was especially horrible when displayed by a child to a parent, or by a child to a sibling. In the Leir story it was nicely contrasted with the loving care provided by the wronged and outcast daughter.

As we suggest in the Appendix (p. 119), Shakespeare would doubtless have heard of the senility of Brian Annesley, a gentleman pensioner of Queen Elizabeth, and of the loving care he had received from his youngest daughter, Cordell, a real-life Cordelia who had followed the example of her legendary namesake. (Presumably her parents knew the Leir story.) It may have been his knowledge of Annesley that made Shakespeare deviate from all the written sources, in none of which Lear goes mad.

Shakespeare rejected the happy ending of the source-play, either because he was aware that this was not the real end of the story, or because in 1605 he did not wish to write a tragi-comedy. Four or five years later, when he was writing *The Winter's Tale* and *Cymbeline*, it became his favourite genre. But a gap in time of some fifteen years, necessary for the reconciliation of Leontes and Hermione, and cemented by the marriage of their daughter to the son of the wronged Polixenes, would have been less acceptable if it were to end with the suicide of an aunt. The suicide of a saintly woman was dramatically impossible. Moreover, if Lear was to be fully aware of the tragic results of his initial error, Cordelia's death, the ultimate result, must come before his own.

We know from many examples that Shakespeare often consulted more than one source.[3] He did this, not for the sake of scholarly or historical accuracy, since in most cases this could hardly apply, but as a stimulus to his imagination. In addition to *King Leir*, therefore, he consulted three, and possibly as many as five, versions of the story. The brief accounts given in Holinshed's *Chronicles* and in Spenser's *The Faerie Queene* (II.x.27–32) he knew already. 'The Complaint of Cordilla', written by John Higgins in *A Mirror for Magistrates,* he may also have read earlier, since he had used *A Mirror* as source material for some of his history plays.

The evidence that Shakespeare consulted these sources was collected by W. W. Greg and other scholars.[4] It consists partly in the use of incidents peculiar to one source. One example is the scene (IV.7) in which Lear and Cordelia kneel to each other, which is based on the corresponding scene in the source-play (see p. 102). Sometimes the evidence consists of verbal resemblances. In Holinshed's *Chronicles*, Cordelia commits suicide with a knife, and there is a picture of the incident. In *A Mirror for Magistrates,* too, she stabs herself. But in *The Faerie Queene* she hangs herself. Here Shakespeare is closest to Spenser: Cordelia is hanged, though not by herself. It is Gonerill who stabs herself.

The influence of Holinshed's brief account was, in fact, slight. The strongest link between chronicle and play is a passage which comes before the account of Leir's reign, where there is a description of the fight between Corineus and the giant Gogmagog at Dover, 'whereof the place was named long after *the fall or leape of Gogmagog*, but afterwards it was called *the fall of Dover*'. Gloucester had to go to Dover to meet Lear, and Shakespeare may have seen Dover cliffs when his company visited the town, but the choice of this cliff by Gloucester for his suicide attempt was probably suggested by this passage in the *Chronicles*, especially as Edgar's account of the imaginary fiend seems to have been influenced by Holinshed's description of the giant.

Higgins uses the name Albany and gives the sisters the same husbands as Shakespeare. His King of France deemed 'that vertue was of dowries all the best'; and Shakespeare's France declares that Cordelia 'is herself a dowry'. Cordilla contrasts her former life as princess and queen with her life in prison, a 'place where thieves do dwell,/From dainty beds of down, to be of straw full fain'. So Shakespeare's Cordelia pities not herself but Lear, when she asks:

> ... and wast thou *fain*, poor father,
> To hovel thee with swine and *rogues* forlorn
> In short and musty *straw*?

Greg listed forty echoes of the old play, and Bullough added others. Some may be coincidences, and others are questionable; but enough remain to provide proof that Shakespeare was well acquainted with the old play. Indeed, the echoes suggest a long acquaintance rather than a recent reading. There is no doubt, for example, that Perillus's attack on Goneril was remembered by Shakespeare, perhaps unconsciously:

> Nay, peace, thou monster, shame unto thy sex,
> Thou fiend in likeness of a human creature.

Leir asks Ragan, 'Knowest thou these letters?' – letters which she snatches and tears. So Shakespeare's Albany (IV.2) compares Gonerill with a fiend, speaks of her shame, tells her not to 'be-monster her feature', and admits that her woman's shape shields her. Then, much later, in the last scene of the play, he shows her the letter she had written to Edmund, revealing her murderous intentions:

13

> Thou worse than any name, read thine own evil.
> No tearing, lady! I perceive you know it.
>   ... Most monstrous! O!
> Knowest thou this paper?

Shakespeare's omissions from the old play are equally significant. He makes no mention of the recent death of Leir's wife; he omits the evil counsellor, Skalliger; he omits the scene in which Goneril and Regan plot against their sister before the love-test; he omits the King of France's courtship in disguise, the attempted murder of Leir and Perillus, and the comic Mumford, whose farcical behaviour parodies the scene where Leir and Cordella kneel to each other.

King Lear has two plots, and the Leir material provided Shakespeare with only one. It will be remembered that in *Hamlet* the hero's task of avenging his father is mirrored by three other instances of sons of murdered fathers: Laertes, whose father has been killed by Hamlet; Fortinbras, whose father had been killed by Hamlet's father; and Pyrrhus, in Aeneas' tale of the fall of Troy, who avenges his father's death on Priam. So in *Othello*, the Moor is not the only jealous character: Roderigo, Iago and Bianca are similarly afflicted. It is not therefore surprising that Shakespeare should seek for a plot which would parallel the ingratitude of Gonerill and Regan, the loving-kindness of Cordelia, and the foolishness of Lear. He already knew Sidney's *Arcadia*, the great prose pastoral romance of the age, and he recalled the episode of the blind Paphlagonian king and his two sons. Sidney called attention to the episode, declaring that it was 'worthy to be remembered for the unused examples therein, as well of true natural goodness as of wretched ungratefulness'. That the children were sons and not daughters must have seemed an advantage, as this provided a desirable variation on the basic theme.

The conversation between the king and his good son is overheard by Pyrocles and Musidorus, the young heroes of the romance, while they are sheltering under a hollow rock from 'so extreme and foul a storm' and the fury of the tempest. They hear that the king, deceived by his bastard son Plexirtus, had ordered the murder of his legitimate son Leonatus, who had escaped and enlisted as a private soldier; that, on hearing that his father had been blinded by Plexirtus, Leonatus had returned to be his guide and comforter; and that the king wanted to kill himself by leaping from a cliff. At this point Shakespeare diverges from Sidney. Plexirtus arrives with forty horsemen to kill his brother; Pyrocles and Musidorus, and later the King of Pontus, join in the battle; Plexirtus is besieged; after crowning Leonatus, the king dies; Plexirtus, pretending to be penitent, is forgiven by his brother, but subsequently attempts to murder him.

Five chapters later, there is a totally unrelated episode which Shakespeare made use of. Plangus, like Edgar, 'subject to that only disadvantage of honest hearts, credulity', is discovered by his father with drawn sword, and his wicked stepmother defends him in such a way as to increase his father's suspicions. In the same way Edmund pretends to defend Edgar.

The final duel between the disguised Edgar and his brother is reminiscent of several fights in *Arcadia*, but the influence is general rather than specific. There are, however, a number of touches, not confined to the sub-plot, that seem to be suggested by Sidney's romance – the suicidal thoughts of Plangus, the idea that we are 'players placed to fill a filthy stage', that we are 'thralls to Fortune's reign' and the 'stars' tennis-balls', and that the cries of the newborn infant are 'the presage of his life'. All these phrases are echoed in *King Lear*.[5]

Whereas the tone of the old play with its happy ending aims merely at pathos, Sidney depicts, it has been said,[6] 'ruthless and sadistic evil tyrannising over the good, whose only resources are resignation, sympathy and kindness'. Those critics are right who argue that the tragic atmosphere of both plots of Shakespeare's play owes much more to *Arcadia* than to the old play. Shakespeare had earlier taken note of Sidney's remarks, in *The Defence of Poesy*, that the function of tragedy was to reveal the ulcers that are covered with tissue, and to make kings fear to be tyrants.

Leonatus, as we have seen, enlists as a soldier; Edgar, with a price on his head, disguises himself as the mad beggar, Poor Tom. This disguise enabled Shakespeare to keep him on stage for most of the play and to allow him to comment on the main plot; but it was also useful in the development of several ideas which were exercising his mind during the writing of the play: the responsibility of the rich for the poor; the essential nature of man; the power of clothing to conceal that essence and to corrupt justice; the wisdom of foolishness, and the sanity hidden in madness. These are all exemplified in the third act of the play, the storm having been suggested by the opening of the episode in *Arcadia*.

Yet a mere Bedlam beggar might have proved tedious. Edgar pretends to be possessed by devils and his chatter adds another dimension to the play, one which was of topical interest. The material for Edgar's speeches was largely taken from Samuel Harsnet's *Declaration of Egregious Popishe Impostures*, published in 1603 but concerned with bogus exorcisms which had taken place years earlier. Harsnet was chaplain to the Bishop of London and he ended his career as Archbishop of York. He had already published a pamphlet on the fraudulent exorcisms of John Darrell, and the purpose of both pamphlets was to discourage the conversions obtained by puritans and papists by exposing their false claims. The probability is that the priests believed what they were doing, but were self-deceived. Harsnet, perhaps because he had been a reader of plays for the bishop, showed himself well acquainted with the theatre, and he treated the exorcisms as a savage farce. He took an unseemly delight in the gruesome details, especially those with a sexual flavour; but he had an effective satirical style, modelled perhaps on that of Thomas Nashe, and plenty of coarse energy. One of the priests mentioned in the book had been at the Stratford-upon-Avon grammar school, and it has been surmised that this accounts for Shakespeare's interest in the book. It is more likely, I think, that his interest was kindled by his knowledge that Harsnet read plays for censorship purposes, and it is possible that he encountered him in that capacity.

Shakespeare took not merely the names of the devils mentioned in Act III – Fraterretto, Modo, Mahu, Hobbididence and the rest – from Harsnet's book, but much more besides. The substance of Poor Tom's speeches and many other details of the storm-scenes can be found scattered through Harsnet's pages, as the following rearranged phrases will demonstrate:

> to wade through a brook ... a new halter and two blades of knives, did leave the same upon the gallery floor ... whirlwind ... devil-blasting ... sprite-blasting ... How dost thou vex me? ... pendulous in the air ... his hair curled up ... the spirit of Pride went out in the form of a peacock, the spirit of Sloth in the likeness of an ass; the spirit of Envy in the similitude of a dog; the spirit of Gluttony in the form of a wolf ... the Prince of hell.

Some speeches of Poor Tom in which he offers moral advice ('Obey thy parents, keep thy word justly; swear not; commit not with man's sworn spouse; set not thy sweet heart on proud array', etc.) seem marginally more appropriate to a victim of Darrell's exorcisms; but the scenes nevertheless brilliantly capture the atmosphere of the Catholic exorcisms as described by Harsnet. One characteristic is omitted, however, to reappear later in the play when Lear inveighs against the lustfulness of women (IV.6).

One other source of *King Lear* remains to be mentioned, though it contributed nothing to the plot: namely Florio's translation of Montaigne's essays, published in 1603, a year or two before Shakespeare began to write the play. In the first place, Florio seems to have extended Shakespeare's already large vocabulary. There are more than a hundred words in *King Lear* not before used by Shakespeare, and he could have picked these up from Florio's translation. Secondly, and more importantly, there are a number of echoes of Florio's phrases. 'Necessity must first pinch you by the throat' is telescoped into 'Necessity's sharp pinch'; 'Frustrate the Tyrant's cruelty' was echoed in 'When misery could beguile the tyrant's rage/And frustrate his proud will'. 'Mangled estate ... gored' may be compared with 'gored state', and 'depositary and guardian' with 'my guardians, my depositaries'.

These echoes merely indicate Shakespeare's familiarity with Florio's translation. More significant are the many ideas Montaigne and Shakespeare held in common (or at least ideas held by Shakespeare's characters) either because the two writers were temperamentally akin, or, more probably, because when he was writing *King Lear* Shakespeare was fresh from a delighted perusal of the essays. Theodore Spencer believed that Shakespeare's tragic sense of life was caused, at least in part, by the impact of the political realism of Machiavelli, the revolutionary ideas of Copernicus, and the views of Montaigne on the nature of man in relation to the animal kingdom.

Montaigne declared that 'we must be besotted ere we can become wise'; that 'the weakness of our judgement helps us more than our strength ... and our blindness more than our clear-sighted eyes'; and that 'our wisdom is less wise than our folly'. (This is close to the position of Erasmus in *Praise of Folly*, which Shakespeare had also read.) Montaigne pointed out that 'our senses are ... many times dulled by the passions of the mind' (cf. III.4.11 and IV.6.5). He mentions an adulterous judge who sentences an adulterer, as the would-be adulterer, Angelo, sentences Claudio. He speaks of the way ladies blush 'at hearing that named which they nothing fear to do' (cf. Lear's diatribe on female sexuality in IV.6). There are many passages in the essays which contrast man's vulnerability with the protection afforded by nature to animals. Man, he said, 'is the only forsaken and outcast creature, naked on the bare earth ... having nothing to cover and arms himself withal but the spoil of others; whereas Nature hath clad and mantled all other creatures, some with husks ... with wool ... with hides ... and with silk ... whereas man only (Oh silly wretched man) can neither go, nor speak, nor shift, nor feed himself, unless it be to whine and weep only, except he be taught'. In a similar passage Montaigne uses the word 'sophisticated', as Lear, commenting on Poor Tom, cries: 'Ha! here's three on 's are sophisticated; thou art the thing itself'.

In the Appendix (p. 120), we point out that Shakespeare repeated some details of the mad-scenes of *Titus Andronicus* in *King Lear*. Marcus kills a fly with gilded wings; a gilded fly lechers in Lear's sight (IV.6.112). Titus gets Lucius to shoot an arrow (cf. IV.6.87), he solicits the gods for justice (cf. III.2.49ff), he produces an imaginary document (cf. IV.6.137) and uses the words 'I know thee well enough', as Lear does (cf. IV.6.178).

These, then, were the heterogeneous materials at Shakespeare's disposal, and doubtless there were others of which we know nothing. Those we do know, as we have seen, included the greatest poem of the age (*The Faerie Queene*), the best essays (Montaigne's) and the finest prose fiction (*Arcadia*), together with an old-fashioned play, a historical chronicle, a 'complaint' from the popular, if dreary, *A Mirror for Magistrates*, a satirical pamphlet, and possibly the real-life story of Cordell Annesley's care for her senile father. The task of creating a unity from these diverse materials was plainly a formidable one; and some critics have argued that Shakespeare did not wholly succeed. Allardyce Nicoll suggested that, whether through exhaustion or haste, Shakespeare 'had failed to think out the possibilities of *King Lear*'; another critic complained of the play's 'loose, episodic structure'; and Bradley[7] compiled a long list of complaints and faults, even doubting whether the advantages of the sub-plot outweighed the disadvantages. There is no need to discuss here Bradley's eighteen criticisms, since they are all of inconsistencies and improbabilities which may be apparent to a reader but would not be noticed in the theatre. They are faults only if judged by the standards of naturalistic drama.

One example is typical. Bradley asks why Gloucester insists on travelling to Dover for the purpose of committing suicide. The simplest reason is theatrical: Shakespeare wanted all his characters to congregate at Dover for the last act, and that is where the French army has landed. A stronger reason is thematic: the meeting of Lear and Gloucester is necessary to bring out the double paradox of the madman who is wiser than when he was supposedly sane, and the blind man who sees more clearly than when he had his eyes. But Gloucester's journey can be defended even on the psychological level. In the traumatic scene of his blinding he is driven to confess that he has sent the king to Dover; Regan and Cornwall shout the question thrice: 'Wherefore to Dover?' To Gloucester's terrified mind, Dover seems a place of sanctuary. He does not yet know that Edmund has betrayed him and that Edgar, the outcast fugitive, is innocent. He does not know that he is to be blinded; he has no intention at this point of committing suicide. But the reiteration of 'Dover' puts him in mind of the cliff when, after his blinding, suicide seems preferable to living.

Shakespeare's choice of the episode from *Arcadia* for his sub-plot meant that he was now provided with a perfect parallel, perfect because not too exact, with sons substituted for daughters, two children instead of three. Sidney, however, with a vagueness allowable to a spoken and selective narrative, gives no details of Plexirtus' deception of his father. Shakespeare therefore amplified this part of the story from the tale of Plangus. He modified the tale in other ways. Whereas the Paphlagonian king speaks of his mistress as 'that base woman, my concubine', Gloucester still has pleasant memories of his association with Edmund's mother. She was fair, and 'there was good sport at his making'. Some critics suppose that Edmund's overhearing of these words motivated his later actions. But he had a much stronger motive (see pp. 54–5). The second alteration is that although Shakespeare makes Edmund responsible for Gloucester's betrayal, he is not present at the blinding. Another significant alteration is that Edmund is genuinely moved by Edgar's account of his father's sufferings and tries to do some good while he lies dying, whereas Plexirtus only pretends to be sorry for his misdeeds, with Leonatus still as credulous as Edgar was at the beginning of the play.

The Paphlagonian king realizes his errors after he has been blinded. Gloucester expresses it epigrammatically: 'I stumbled when I saw'. Shakespeare needed a thematic parallel to this in the main plot, and he found it in the madness of Lear. In no previous version of the story does Lear become insane. The idea may have come from Shakespeare's feeling that ingratitude was worse than any vice, and the horror of it was intensified when a son or daughter is ungrateful to a parent. He may have picked up hints from Harsnet's *Declaration*, from the Annesley story, or, indeed, from the prevalent notion that mad people have moments of illumination – 'reason in madness'.

Shakespeare already had Armin to play the part of a sage Fool. We do not know at what point in his planning of the play he decided to have Edgar disguise himself as Poor Tom, nor at what point he amplified the role by making him a demoniac. But here we can see the way in which he came to envisage the juxtaposition of three kinds of madness – a quartet, indeed, for the elements in Act III reflect Lear's madness, as everyone recognizes (see p. 77). As we have noticed, there is a storm from which Musidorus and Pyrocles shelter. Harsnet speaks of one so 'violent, boisterous and big, as that he will ruffle, rage, and hurl in the air . . . and blow down steeples, trees, may-poles'; and one of the demoniacs who lay in the fields 'was scared with lightning and thunder'.

As we have suggested, Shakespeare must have decided early on – as soon as he had determined on a tragedy – not to have Cordelia commit suicide, and not to have a long gap in the action while her nephews grow up. Even more important, dramatically, was to have Cordelia die before her father. We must see, and the tragic hero must realize, the ultimate result of his initial error. But if Cordelia is not to kill herself, someone must kill her. Her sisters hate her simply because her goodness shows up their wickedness, but as they have already defeated her by getting her share of the kingdom, Shakespeare went elsewhere for her murderer, and he went to the sub-plot. All Edmund's actions, except the last, are prompted by self-interest. He has no personal animosity against Cordelia. His ultimate aim is apparently to be king over a united Britain, an ambition kindled by the rivalry of Gonerill and Regan and increased, we may assume, by the death of Cornwall, which leaves a power vacuum. The continued existence of Cordelia, even an imprisoned Cordelia, with the power of France and the sympathy of Albany on her side, would be a threat to this ambition. Plexitrus does become king; to succeed to a mere dukedom is not enough for Edmund. Ironically, his murder of Cordelia smoothes the path of the reluctant Edgar to the throne.

It would have outraged the audience if Shakespeare had allowed Gonerill and Regan to survive after the murder of Cordelia. It is only with the advent of the Theatre of Cruelty in the present century that such an outrage could be deemed acceptable. Appropriately, the evil sisters are destroyed by their own passions. Their sexual rivalry is not suggested in any version of the Lear story, although in the old play they are both jealous of Cordella's beauty. Shakespeare, in altering the characters of Goneril and Ragan, was also bound to stress the sexual attractiveness of Edmund. This is hinted at in the opening scene, and made apparent in his first soliloquy in which he boasts that the lust that led to his conception, the 'good sport at his making', has made his dimensions and shape as attractive as those of legitimate children, and that he has 'more composition and fierce quality'. The mental and physical superiority of bastards had been argued in one of the paradoxes of Ortensio Landi (see Commentary, I.2), and one of John Donne's problems, written but then not yet published, was entitled 'Why have Bastards best Fortune'.

Before the end of the play and before his fatal duel, Edmund finds himself in a dilemma. Gonerill and Regan are fighting for him, and he does not know which marriage will best further his ambition. Even when Cornwall is removed from the scene and Regan becomes an accessible widow, he knows that Gonerill will do anything to prevent his marriage to her rival. Gonerill, indeed, wants Edmund to kill Albany: he proposes to leave the deed to her.

Shakespeare adds a further complication – the threat of war between Cornwall and Albany. An actual war would not have served his purpose, and it would have distracted attention from the central issues of the play. The threat is rumoured at II.1.10; it is ignored when Gonerill meets Regan later in the act; it is mentioned obscurely by Kent in III.1 and by

Gloucester in III.3; and it is presumably aborted by the death of Cornwall. We are not told the cause of the quarrel. Shakespeare may have wished merely to indicate that a civil war was the inevitable or at least probable result of the division of the kingdom; but it was also a way of distancing the well-meaning Albany from the ill-intentioned Cornwall, especially as they may have seemed much alike in the first scene of the play. Albany's gradual realization that he has married an evil and masterful woman is revealed in a series of subtle touches.

The killing of Cornwall in the midst of his blinding of Gloucester, an action Cornwall continues even after receiving his death-wound, is an appropriate nemesis which enables Albany to see in it the operation of divine punishment; but with characteristic ambiguity Shakespeare puts the instrument of punishment in the hands of a nameless servant who is revolted by his master's cruelty. The servant is stabbed from behind by Regan, and his body is thrown on a dunghill; but his brave action is not merely the first check to the triumphant progress of evil; it leads to the eventual downfall of Gonerill and Regan, of Edmund, and incidentally of Oswald. Cornwall's other two servants are not heroic like their fellow; but they have decent and humane feelings, and Shakespeare uses them to express the audience's horror at the scene they have just beheld. (That the lines do not appear in the Folio is the strongest argument against Shakespeare's responsibility for all the cuts.)

In the final scene Shakespeare uses various means to increase the tension. Instead of the defeat of Plexirtus in a regular battle, we are given the duel in which the disguised Edgar challenges the victorious warrior, Edmund, and wins against all odds. Those members of the audience who remembered the old play would half expect a happy ending; and when Edmund is moved by the account of his father's suffering, they may feel sure that the reprieve of Lear and Cordelia will come in time. Edmund speaks at last, but five minutes too late. Albany's prayer is ignored by the gods: in the world of absolute tragedy there is no place for divine intervention. Some critics feel that Shakespeare allowed too great an element of chance; but there is always an element of chance in all Shakespeare's tragedies, from the quarantine which prevents Romeo from receiving a message from Friar Lawrence, to Emilia's arrival in the last scene of *Othello*, two minutes too late to prevent the murder of Desdemona. Edmund's delay in speaking is discussed below (p. 109–10).

In some such way as this Shakespeare fused together the different elements of his sources. The use of poetry to perfect the fusion is discussed later in 'Themes and Images'. He made the characters of the Sidney story play a dominant role in the main plot. This was necessary because, after

21

the division of the kingdom, Lear himself does not act: he is acted upon. Edmund, by contrast, in his quest for sovereignty, is continuously active, achieving first his brother's banishment, becoming his father's heir, enlisting in Cornwall's service, betraying Gloucester, then, uneasily poised between the two royal duchesses, becoming the commander-in-chief of Regan's troops, and finally ordering the execution of Lear and Cordelia. Edgar performs seven or eight roles before he ends up as the future king. Even Gloucester, credulous and spineless at first, does finally decide to support the king, communicates with the 'enemy', and assists Lear's escape from a death-plot. (This is mentioned in passing (III.6.87), not dramatized as it had been in the old play.)

It is sometimes said that *Arcadia* and the Leir story belong to such different eras and different genres that Shakespeare in combining them did not quite succeed in papering the cracks. In reading the play we may perhaps notice that the Gloucester story belongs to a later date, and that the Bedlam beggar throws us forward to a problem of Shakespeare's lifetime; but I have never known audiences notice any disparity, nor even, I may add, any member of the cast in the two productions with which I have been associated.

Other critics have made the very opposite accusation. They admire the extraordinary skill of the dramatist, but feel that in this play he is too clever by half. Gide, after watching Olivier in the title role, declared that it was the worst of Shakespeare's tragedies, that in it there is 'nothing that is not intentional, arbitrary, forced ... Art triumphs' – by which Gide meant that it triumphed at the expense of life. John Middleton Murry, who was disturbed by the sex-nausea displayed by Lear, complained nevertheless that the play was 'cold and inhuman'. In spite of the admittedly great pains Shakespeare took in its construction, it remained an artefact, inferior to *Coriolanus*. These critics are happily in a minority, as heretical as those who complain of the looseness of its construction. In the opinion of most modern critics, *King Lear* has replaced *Hamlet* as the tragedy that speaks most directly to today's readers and audiences.

Characterization

Throughout the Commentary which follows, the reader's attention is called to speeches and incidents that throw light on the characters. The present chapter, therefore, is designed to be complementary and it discusses them from a different point of view.

The usual method of analysing Shakespeare's characters, employed in countless editions during the present century, is to tabulate what they say and do, and add what other characters say about them. This is a possible method; but it can be misleading, as it starts from the wrong end. Shakespeare did not start by inventing characters, and then search for a suitable plot to embody them. From what has been said in the previous chapter, it will have become apparent that his characters are largely defined, if not circumscribed, by their roles, or by their function in the plot.

The Fool

This definition of a role by circumstance or function is obvious with the Fool, who is basically the traditional fool, a truth-teller. He is also, equally obviously, a splendid part for Armin, fresh from his triumphs in *As You Like It* and *Twelfth Night*. Shakespeare had seen what he could do, so he was given a more important role in *King Lear*, one which (as Keats said) 'gave a finishing touch to the pathos'. Of course Shakespeare added some individualizing touches, such as his pining away after Cordelia's departure, and Armin doubtless added others. Some think he added the prophecy in III.2, absent from the Quarto text, since he was an author as well as an actor. I agree with Joseph Wittreich that Shakespeare himself was responsible for it.

Our impressions of the character depend very largely on the close relationship between him and Lear. Shakespeare does not tell us everything: for example, we are not told what happens to him after the storm-scenes. Nor are we told about his motives; we can only deduce them. In the storm he labours to outjest Lear's injuries, but in earlier scenes his devotion to Cordelia makes him harp on Lear's foolishness in disinheriting her. Does this help to drive Lear mad? Or does the Fool believe that his master can be saved only by dragging the guilt into full consciousness? (See Commentary on I.4.91ff., II.4, III.2, III.6, V.3.)

23

Kent

Once Shakespeare had decided to model Kent on Perillus in the old play, and had added the sentence of banishment because of his outspoken criticism of his tyrannical master, and his return in disguise to serve Lear until death, the outlines of his character were determined. In disguise he could be the plain, blunt man, without the inhibitions imposed by custom and society. He does not try to conceal his contempt for Oswald and his dislike of Cornwall and Regan; and, as the audience shares his contempt and dislike, he always has them on his side, however outrageously he behaves. Shakespeare adds a number of individualizing characteristics – his stoicism in the stocks, his love of Cordelia, his embracing of Edgar after shunning him as Poor Tom, his pathetic attempt to get the king to understand that he was the disguised Caius. Even his remark on the difference between Lear's three daughters – 'It is the stars that govern our condition' – is revealing. (See Commentary on I.1, II.2.)

It was Maurice Morgann (in his essay on Falstaff) who first pointed out the way in which Shakespeare set up conflicting impressions of his characters, and since we all have such conflicting impressions of our friends and acquaintances, Shakespeare's characters seem to be more lifelike than those of any other dramatist. In *King Lear* some of the conflicting impressions would be caused by the contrast between the original story and Shakespeare's deviations from it, thus cheating the expectations of those members of the audience who were familiar with the old play. Then, as I have recently expressed the matter,[1]

The story was not merely well known and legendary, but archetypal and mythical, so that the audience has the feeling, as it watches the love-test or the scene where the proud king and the proud daughter kneel to each other, that they are witnessing, one might almost say, re-enacting, something that happened 'A great while since, a long long time ago'. Such a feeling is bound to affect, if only subliminally, an audience's reactions to the characters of the play. Lear and Gloucester, Goneril and Regan, are vividly realized characters, with different speech patterns, characters so delusively real that they have attracted the attention of psychoanalysts. On the other hand, they are mythological figures, as fated as Oedipus to fulfil their destinies.

Oswald

Keats said that Shakespeare had as much delight in depicting the villain Iago as the heroine Imogen, or, as he might have put it, as much delight in depicting Edmund as Edgar. However evil or unpleasant the characters, they speak from their own point of view. We tend to look at Oswald through the eyes of Kent and Lear, and think of him as foppish, effeminate, cowardly, and a minister to his mistress's vices, 'something between a pimp and a gigolo'. He is all these things, but if he were to write his own epitaph, it would surely be: 'Here lies a loyal and faithful servant'. He refuses to let Regan open Gonerill's letter; he is killed in carrying out his mistress's wishes; and his last thought is to get his killer to deliver Gonerill's letter to Edmund.

Edmund

Edmund's humour, cleverness, courage and virility arouse some sympathy in spite of his evil deeds. Even his illegitimacy goes some way to excuse his determination to succeed in spite of it. But it is significant that he and Cornwall are drawn to each other at their first meeting, evil attracting evil. He outwits his brother by his cunning, betrays his father to Cornwall so that he can succeed to the earldom, and, aiming ultimately at the crown, he orders the execution of Lear and Cordelia. As he is mortally wounded, he is unexpectedly moved by the account of his father's sufferings and death – unexpectedly, because up till then his motives have been entirely selfish. He hints that Edgar's story 'may perchance do good'. The deaths of Lear and Cordelia cannot any longer serve his ambition, but he does not speak until the dead bodies of Gonerill and Regan are brought in. On one level the delay may be due to the dramatist's decision to prevent a happy ending; but there are two valid psychological explanations. Either we may assume that Edmund was loyal to Gonerill, who was involved in the plan to murder Lear and Cordelia, and that he could not speak while she was still alive; or else he was able to act disinterestedly for the first time because he realized that he, the illegitimate and deprived child, had won the love of two princesses: 'Yet Edmund was beloved'.

(See I.2, II.1, V.1, V.3.)

Edgar

Some critics believe that Edgar has no character at all, that he is purely functional: he has to be a dupe at the beginning of the play, and later a guide and avenger, while throughout he has to act as a commentator and chorus. Leo Kirschbaum declared that to 'make a psychological unity of Edgar's various roles is a misguided endeavour'.[2] But Shakespeare's choric figures (for example, Horatio in *Hamlet*, Enobarbus in *Antony and Cleopatra*) are never merely that. Beneath the various roles he assumes, Edgar is a coherent and developing character. He develops, indeed, as most people do, by role-playing. If we compare the stooge who is so easy a victim of his brother's cunning with the king-elect of the last scene of the play, it seems a miraculous transformation. But, taken step by step and scene by scene, the development seems perfectly credible.

Edgar begins by assuming that other people are as honest as himself – the Elizabethans believed that 'Your noblest natures are most credulous'. He suspects some villain has done him wrong, without suspecting that the villain is his own brother. To escape capture he disguises himself as a Bedlam beggar, someone who is at the very bottom of the social ladder. someone who can never even put his foot on the lowest rung. In that role he learns what it is like to be poor and despised, disdained even by dogs. This disguise, as we have seen, is complicated by his pretence that he is possessed by devils, and this enables him to fabricate a past for himself. His inherent nobility and natural goodness are revealed in his reaction to Lear's madness, which makes his own suffering seem bearable: 'How light and portable my pain seems now,/When that which makes me bend makes the King bow'.

He thinks he has reached the very bottom, that any change is bound to be an improvement, only to be confronted with the blind father he still loves, and to realize that he had not till then reached the worst. He willingly agrees to guide his father and determines to prevent his suicide. At Dover, after Gloucester has failed to kill himself, Edgar perforce adopts another persona, that of a poor countryman who, 'by the art of known and feeling sorrows', is 'pregnant to good pity' – a true account of his own experience. When Oswald enters, Edgar adopts a more rustic accent in case he should be recognized. Gonerill's letter enables him to denounce Edmund to Albany and to offer his challenge. He takes part in the battle, reveals his identity to his father, defeats Edmund before revealing himself, forgives him, and emerges at the end as the one man who has the strength, wisdom and compassion necessary for kingship.

Some recent critics, however, find Edgar irritating. S. L. Goldberg, for example, thinks that Shakespeare himself 'felt slightly irritated by such adept, talkative, but fundamentally self-protective moralism'.[3] Others deplore his remark to Edmund on his father's adultery, particularly objectionable because the words are spoken so soon after Gloucester's death (V.3.168–71):

> The gods are just, and of our pleasant vices
> Make instruments to plague us:
> The dark and vicious place where thee he got
> Cost him his eyes.

Both comments, however, are misconceived. The moralism would not have been regarded by a Jacobean audience or readers as smug and self-protective. Shakespeare, as far as we know, did not regard it ironically, although Edgar's hopes are continually dashed by events. As for the comment on Gloucester's blinding, we have to remember that Edgar has treated his father with loving care and forgiveness; but he knows, and sternly asserts, that the act of adultery had led to the birth of his bastard brother, and hence to Edmund's crimes and Gloucester's blinding; and the audience knows that the chain of evil is not yet complete. There are to be four more victims. Elton suggests that Edgar makes the remark to comfort his dying brother, who accepts stoically that the wheel has come full circle. One other point should be made. Nearly all the characters make statements about the gods. In the total design of the play, Gloucester's idea that the gods torture us for their sport needs to be answered by his son's declaration that the gods are just. But it is not necessary to assume that Shakespeare subscribed to either view.

(See II.3, III.4, III.6, IV.1, V.2, V.3.)

Gloucester

Gloucester is introduced in the opening lines of the play, complacently referring to the good sport he had with Edmund's mother. He is absent from the stage during the love-test, and makes no immediate comment when he returns; but, as we learn in the next scene, he is disturbed by Kent's banishment, by the King of France's anger (for some unspecified cause), and by the reduction in Lear's power. He is easily deceived by Edmund and jumps with absurd rapidity to the conclusion that the son he has loved for years is a villain. His belief in astrology, which he shares with Kent in the play, and with many intelligent Elizabethans, is derided by Edmund, but it does not in itself prove that he is stupidly superstitious. He admires the 'noble and true-hearted Kent', and is worried by the quarrel between Lear and his daughters. He protests at the stocking of 'Caius' and expresses his sympathy. But at the end of Act II, after an ineffective protest, he locks his doors on the king. Then, despite the danger to himself, he goes to succour Lear, and eventually declares, 'Though I die for it, the King, my old master, must be relieved'. He has been driven more by loyalty and decency than by self-interest to take sides. This proves to be a fatal step, because he informs Edmund. In the blinding-scene he displays the courage of desperation in denouncing the cruelty of Gonerill and Regan, threatening them with divine vengeance. It is in this scene that he is made to realize his folly in trusting Edmund – and it is this and his misjudgement of Edgar, as much as his blinding, which makes him resolve to commit suicide. In his most famous words, which some critics have tried to make the keynote of the play, he declares that the gods are sadistic monsters, the pattern for Regan and Cornwall; but when next we meet him he refers to the gods as 'ever-gentle'. His religion is entirely subjective and superstitious; and this Edgar realizes when he makes him believe that he has been saved by a miracle. Thereafter, with some lapses into despair, Gloucester accepts the necessity of stoical endurance. His encounter with the mad Lear provokes feelings which are a mixture of pity and envy – pity for a ruined piece of nature, envy of the insensibility of madness that 'by wrong imaginations' prevents him from feeling his woes. In the last act, when he learns that Edgar has been his guide and comforter, Gloucester, exhausted by his sufferings, dies of joy.

(See II.4.291ff., III.7, IV.1.15, IV.6.)

Gonerill and Regan

Gonerill and Regan are not at first, as Edith Sitwell pointed out, 'in their own view, nor from the world's point of view, wicked'. They tell themselves that 'they are but doing their duty towards their father and towards the world'. In the first scene of the play they seem very much alike, two beautiful hypocrites who outwit their good sister. In their fulsome speeches to Lear they both use the same metallic imagery, as though love were simply a commodity. Regan merely echoes her sister. It becomes apparent that this is a characteristic of their relationship, except in relation to Edmund. They join together in adopting a tone of moral rebuke to Cordelia, who knows, as apparently Lear does not, what they are really like. When they are left alone, their realistic appraisal of Lear's character, their accusation that he is in his dotage, though largely true, stands in stark contrast to the love they have professed. The plan they adopt (although not defined as yet) is clearly Gonerill's. Now they have the power – significantly, their husbands are not mentioned – they are determined to ignore the conditions Lear had laid down: the retention of a retinue of a hundred knights and the monthly alternation of hospitality. By making their father feel that he is unwelcome, they can force him to reduce his retinue. Of course they have plausible excuses, and Gonerill can adopt at will a lofty moral, almost puritanical, tone; but there is no need to believe that there is any truth in her denunciation of Lear's knights, though Komisajevski and other directors have been taken in by her. It has been made clear by her instructions to Oswald – to be as negligent as possible – that her attack on the knights is part of her strategy. The demand that Lear should reduce his retinue leads to his curse of Gonerill

28

and of her potential offspring. This is so dreadful that some actresses have thought that this is the point at which Gonerill changes from being a cold-hearted hypocrite to one with temptations of parricide; Bradley, however, declares that her father's curse is nothing to her. It can be played either way.

Lear, as Gonerill intends, leaves before the expiration of a month, believing, despite the Fool's warnings, that Regan will be kind to him, and will be deeply shocked by Gonerill's behaviour. She proves to be even more brutal. It is she who, on the subject of the knights, asks the final question: 'What need one?', and it is she who orders Gloucester to bar his doors.

Gonerill is not present at the blinding of Gloucester, although the blinding is at her suggestion. Regan is present. She takes a sadistic delight in interrogating the prisoner, in plucking him by the beard, in inciting Cornwall to gouge out the second eye, in stabbing the servant in the back, in informing Gloucester that he has been betrayed by Edmund, and in her final order: 'Go thrust him out at gates and let him smell/His way to Dover.'

In the rest of the play she is violently jealous of Gonerill, but she does not suspect that she is being poisoned. Bradley speaks of her 'venomous meanness, which is almost as hateful as her cruelty. She is the most hideous human being (if she is one) that Shakespeare ever drew.' Perhaps the doubts expressed in the parenthesis would not have occurred to Bradley if he had lived to hear of the horrors of the present century. Swinburne forestalled Bradley in his doubts when he remarked that only in one case did Shakespeare fail to prevent a character from 'passing from the abnormal into the monstrous ... In Regan only would it be impossible to find a touch or trace of anything less vile than it was devilish.' But Barker thought that Shakespeare saw 'little to choose between hot lust and murdering hand and the hard heart, in which all is rooted'.

Despite the knowledge that Gonerill is a murderous adulteress, audiences greatly prefer her to Regan. This is partly because of her patriotic rhetoric when she upbraids Albany for his failure to mobilize against the French invaders. It is, as Johnson defined it, 'the last refuge of a scoundrel'. She is replying to Albany's denunciation of her wickedness, though he does not yet know that she has taken a lover and plotted his death. Albany's scruples can be seen as weakness. 'Where I could not be honest,' he says, 'I never yet was valiant.' In the circumstances his duty is by no means clear, and Gonerill arouses more sympathy than she should.

Part of the trouble is that Albany's part has been damaged by severe Folio cuts, and he is seldom played by an actor with enough authority.

But more serious is the way in which patriotism often drives out moral considerations (as anyone who has lived through a world war will admit), and Shakespeare, as we have seen, always gives the devil his due. There is something to admire in Gonerill's defiance when she knows she is defeated: 'the laws are mine, not thine./Who can arraign me for't?'

Cordelia

The characters of all three sisters are largely determined by the story Shakespeare chose to dramatize; but, as we have seen, he adds a number of individualizing characteristics. He shows that Gonerill has inherited her father's pride and arrogance; and Cordelia, as Barker says, 'has more than a touch of her father in her. She is as proud as he is, and as obstinate, for all her sweetness and her youth.' Although her behaviour in the first scene is caused by her disgust with her sisters and by her inability to barter love for profit, she is also naturally reticent in speaking of her inmost feelings. This is apparent again in the scene of reunion. Before her father wakes she pours out her love for him; but as soon as Lear can hear her, her eloquence is reduced to monosyllables. It is as though Cordelia, and perhaps Shakespeare himself, were becoming embarrassed by the inevitable falsity of language, as she had been before in the love-test scene.

When Lear and Cordelia are taken off to prison, she is, characteristically, sorry for him rather than for herself. She is proud to be able to 'outfrown false Fortune's frown', though with ineffable scorn she asks Edmund (or possibly her father): 'Shall we not see these daughters and these sisters?' These are her last words. She realizes that Lear's expectation of a joyful life in prison is an illusion: she guesses they will be in death-row.

(See Commentary on I.1.33ff., IV.3, IV.4, IV.7.)

Albany and Cornwall

Albany and Cornwall are a pair of characters who are nicely contrasted, as they are on opposite sides of the moral fence. We do not immediately realize this. In the first scene they are indistinguishable consorts of the two princesses; but, as the play progresses, the difference between them becomes apparent. Cornwall, for example, wholeheartedly approves of the humiliation of Lear by Regan, he enlists the scoundrel Edmund to his side, and he positively enjoys the torture of Gloucester. Albany, although shocked by Lear's curse of Gonerill and of their children, and although still under the spell of her beauty and of her regal authority, begins to criticize her treatment of Lear – still comparatively mild – and is snubbed for his pains as one who is more condemned for his lack of wisdom than praised for his 'harmful mildness'. Humane sentiments are regarded by her and her associates as vices rather than virtues.

Albany is absent from the stage for the whole of the second and third acts – nearly 1,400 lines – and when we next see him his character has undergone a transformation. He has been horrified by the treatment of their father by Gonerill and Regan, his great love for Gonerill has been replaced by disgust at her true character, and he denounces her with a moral authority we might not have suspected. The threatened war between the dukes also shows that he has distanced himself from Cornwall, even before he knows of the way Lear has been treated. His immediate understanding of the truth about Gloucester's arrest shows his instinctive goodness; but his belief that if the gods do not intervene to punish human depravity men will prey on each other 'like monsters of the deep', and his conviction that the death of Cornwall while engaged on his most horrible deed is a proof that they have indeed intervened, may seem naive, especially when considered in relation to his later prayer for the safety of Lear and Cordelia. He has to learn that the gods do not (or do not always) intervene to avert the consequences of human folly and wickedness. Nevertheless, in the last act of the play, when Albany learns the full extent of Gonerill's villainy, and is willing to fight Edmund if the challenger fails to arrive, he shows himself to be entirely in control and a very different man from the one whom Gonerill could despise for his gentleness, as his remark on the corpses of Gonerill and Regan illustrates: 'This judgement of the heavens that makes us tremble/Touches us not with pity.' But he is modest. He resigns his power to Lear; and, when Lear dies, he urges Kent and Edgar to rule in the state. (See V.3.296, V.3.317.)

Lear

Lear is in his eighties, and although he is still physically active there is nothing discreditable in his wish to abdicate and prepare himself for death, and there is nothing inherently unwise for a king with no male heir to try to avoid future strife by arranging for the marriage of his daughters and dividing the kingdom between them. Yet the plan proves to be disastrous because of the characters of the daughters and because of flaws in Lear himself. Orwell compared him with Tolstoy, who clung to the power he had ostentatiously renounced. Lear had been flattered so long that he was no longer capable of distinguishing between the genuine and the false: he wished to cling to the illusion of power without the substance; and he still craved love and gratitude. This is the motive for the love-test which is a last-minute addition to the abdication ceremony. Lear does not intend that his daughters' speeches shall alter their shares, already marked on the map. He is foiled by Cordelia's refusal to join in the love-auction; and in his rage he banishes her without a dowry, and banishes Kent for intervening on her behalf.

This was Shakespeare's *donnée*, the initial situation in all versions of the story; and Lear's fatal misjudgement is an integral part of it. His character had to be created to suit the situation, although we may also be made to believe that the situation results from his character. His rage is a measure of his disappointment. He loved Cordelia most, believed his love to be returned, and hoped to spend his remaining years in her loving care. The idea of alternate visits to his other two daughters was not part of his original plan.

When the victorious sisters discuss their father, the audience, although alerted to their hypocrisy by Cordelia and Kent, is likely to agree with their diagnosis, and with their prognosis (I.1.294–8):

The best and soundest of his time hath been but rash. Then must we look from his age to receive not alone the imperfections of long-ingraffed condition, but therewithal the unruly waywardness that infirm and choleric years bring with them.

Lear, they say, has always been rash and overbearing; now, on the verge of senility, he is likely to become a menace.

During the remainder of the play we are forced to revise our opinion of Lear, partly because we are shown his more attractive side and partly because he himself changes. His affection for the Fool, who continually acts as his sternest critic, is an indication that he has not been entirely ruined by the absolute power which, we are told, corrupts absolutely. His resentment at Gonerill's ingratitude makes him see that Cordelia's fault was small by comparison; 'I did her wrong,' he confesses (I.5.24), and for the first time he has a premonition of madness.

Before the end of the second act, Lear realizes that Regan is worse than Gonerill. He begins to consider man's essential needs: when he was king there was no necessity for such concerns. He prays for patience, but a moment later, in impotent rage, he swears he will be avenged on the unnatural hags, his daughters. His last words in this scene are spoken to the Fool, his loyal supporter and conscience: 'O Fool, I shall go mad!' He does not, however, go mad at once. He addresses the gods and the storm; he seems at times to be the embodiment of the storm, and at other times to feel that the wind and rain are in league with his daughters. He feels compassion for the shivering Fool and also for the poor naked wretches for whose plight he had taken too little care. Then he is confronted with one such naked wretch, Poor Tom; and this is the moment when he really goes mad. 'Didst thou give all to thy daughters?' he asks, and soon afterwards assumes that essential man, man without the sophistications of civilization, is like this.

In the mock trial he takes the Fool in his motley, Poor Tom in his blanket, and his servant Caius to be three judges, and he creates out of nothing the forms of Gonerill and Regan. Although he arraigns them both and is his own witness, he is more deeply concerned with the question: 'Is there any cause in nature that makes these hard hearts?'

After this scene, Lear is absent from the stage for a long period – the last scene of Act III and the first five scenes of Act IV – and we hear that in his lucid intervals, because of his shame, he refuses to see Cordelia. At other times he is crowned with weeds and sings aloud. When we do see him at Dover he is suffering from extraordinary delusions, but these are mingled with moments of insight – his acceptance of the fact that he has been flattered all his life, his attack on the hypocrisy of lecherous women and corrupt judges, his perception that there is one kind of justice for the poor and another for the rich, and, in his 'sermon', his realization that human life is inescapably tragic. It is, as Edgar points out, 'matter and impertinency' (i.e. irrelevancy) mixed.

The scene in the old play in which Leir and his daughter kneel to each other was one Shakespeare had to use; it was perhaps the scene which attracted him to the subject. One could say that the experiences Lear had undergone and the way he had developed since his banishment of Cordelia led up to this scene of reconciliation. The love-test and the kneeling were the two fixed points in the characterization of Lear. The proud king humbles himself and begs forgiveness.

In that scene Lear has regained his sanity, though, as he confesses, he is 'a very foolish fond old man'. In the scene in which he and Cordelia are led off to prison, he has regained much of his vitality. He looks forward with joy to a future of untroubled love, to a continual repetition of the scene of forgiveness, detached from worldly affairs and no longer concerned with thoughts of revenge. The audience soon learns what Cordelia knows already: that their time will be short.

When Lear re-enters, it is with Cordelia's body; and in the final scene he oscillates between hope and despair, so that the audience agrees with Kent that Lear's death is a merciful release:

> He hates him
> That would upon the rack of this tough world
> Stretch him out longer.

In this discussion of the characterization in *King Lear*, it will have become apparent that most of the characters are abnormally good (Cordelia, Edgar, Kent) or atrociously bad (Gonerill, Regan, Cornwall, Edmund, Oswald). This division into black and white is unique in Shakespeare's plays. In *Hamlet*, for example, there is only one really wicked character, and even he tries to repent. In *Macbeth* the hero is a murderer, but not at all in the same black company as the villains in *King Lear*. Only in *Othello* do we have an absolute villain, and Othello calls him a 'demi-devil'. There are, of course, characters in *King Lear* who are betwixt and between. Lear and Gloucester begin as wickedly foolish, but they improve in the course of the play. Others are driven to make a stand against the extreme evil with which they are faced. The turning-point comes for Cornwall's servant half-way through the blinding-scene. Albany turns against his beautiful wife when he realizes what she is like. On the other hand, we can observe the temptation and fall of the captain who agrees to the murder of Lear and Cordelia.

We may note further that the characters are given appropriate attitudes to the beliefs and ideas that crop up in the course of the play. Cordelia and Edgar seem to be natural 'Christians' in a pre-Christian world. The evil characters are all atheists. Gloucester, a nominal believer, veers erratically from the conviction that the gods are cruel to the assumption that they are kindly. Both Lear and Edmund pray to Nature; but to Edmund the word is merely a symbol of his own ruthless ambition. Albany thinks the gods are just and will intervene to protect the righteous and punish the innocent; whether he is convinced of this at the end of the play is somewhat doubtful. In the discussion of imagery in the next chapter, we shall attempt to show that this can also be used to differentiate character.

Shakespeare's poetic method of characterization is not that of a naturalistic dramatist. The nature and development of his major characters are determined largely by the plot and the theme, and the words they speak contribute as much to the overall meaning of the play as to the psychology of the characters. Examples could be found on almost every page of the script. When Lear speaks of 'unaccommodated man' or of the great image of authority, or when Lear and Gloucester quite independently advocate a fairer distribution of wealth, or when Kent asks: 'Is this the promised end?', these are not simply the utterances of the characters. Yet because

of the conflicting impressions we have of them, Shakespeare's characters
seem more alive than the consistent, well-drawn characters of nearly all
other dramatists.

Themes and Images

Several of the main themes of *King Lear* are inherent in the two main stories that Shakespeare combined. The misjudgements of Lear and Gloucester about their children, the dreadful results of their foolishness, and their realization of the truth – gradual in Lear's case, sudden in Gloucester's; the rewarding of the wicked and the punishment of the good children, followed by the ingratitude of the favoured ones and the repayment of good for evil by the maltreated; and the double paradox that Lear becomes wiser after he becomes mad, and that Gloucester has more insight after he has lost the sight of his eyes – all these emerge naturally from the plot.

The paradox is reinforced by the imagery. The numerous images that relate to sight and blindness, as Robert Heilman has demonstrated,[1] are not confined to the Gloucester plot. Lear, for example, prays for the lightnings to dart their 'blinding flames/Into her scornful eyes'. The Fool warns that 'Fathers that wear rags/Do make their children blind'. Lear threatens to pluck out his eyes, as Oedipus had done. Even the winds are described as blind, 'impetuous blasts with eyeless rage'. But the climax of this imagery is to be found in the actual blinding-scene, and its aftermath when Gloucester confesses: 'I stumbled when I saw'.

Although Gonerill, who shares Cornwall's hesitation about killing the alleged traitor, is the first to suggest the plucking-out of his eyes, it seems to be Gloucester's prophecy ('I shall see/The wingèd Vengeance overtake such children') that provokes Cornwall to execute the deed.

Dr Johnson said he was not able to defend 'the extrusion of Gloucester's eyes, which seems an act too horrid to be endured in dramatic exhibition', and he went on to suggest that Shakespeare was pandering to the bad taste of his audience. But was he? J. I. M. Stewart[2] suggested that in this scene there was 'a spilling over, as it were, of physical outrage from imagery into action. And in this lay, perhaps, the chief consideration in favour of staging the blinding.' A mere description of the outrage would not have the same effect; and it was necessary for an audience to be made fully aware of the horror in all its sadistic vileness. An uncensored version of evil is an essential part of the stark contrasts of the world of the play. The scene, moreover, inevitably leads to a rush of sympathy for the victim.

After the blinding, Gloucester realizes that the insensitive rich man will not see because he does not feel; and he says that if only he could touch

Edgar, he would say he had eyes again. Edgar, in his comment on the act that led to Edmund's birth, says that: 'The dark and vicious place where thee he got/Cost him his eyes.' We should remember that blinding was considered by some of Shakespeare's pious contemporaries to be a suitable punishment for the sin of adultery.[3]

The complementary theme of Lear's increased understanding through his increasing madness is supported not so much by the imagery as by the actual development of his thoughts. When he feels the onset of madness, he begins to consider the true needs of human beings; on the verge of insanity, he considers the plight of the naked and outcast (in whom Blake urged us to seek love);[4] while he is raving, he examines the contrast between 'sophisticated', civilized man and man in his essence; he broods on the cause of hardness of heart, whether it is a disease or a sin; he shows that those who administer justice are often as guilty as the criminals they try, and he reveals 'the great image of authority' – 'a dog's obeyed in office'; and he preaches on the inevitable tragedy of human life on 'this great stage of fools'.

These insights – what Edgar calls 'reason in madness' – are linked with the satirical comments of the Fool, and they reflect in some sense the attitude expressed by Erasmus in *Praise of Folly*. As Enid Welsford puts it: 'Lear's tragedy is the investing of the King with motley: it is also the crowning and apotheosis of the Fool.'[5] Richard Moulton pointed out that

the Centrepiece of the play is occupied with the contact of two madnesses, the madness of Lear and the madness of Edgar [i.e. of Poor Tom]; that of Lear gathering up into a climax trains of passion from all the three tragedies of the main plot, and that of Edgar holding a similar position to the three tragedies of the underplot. Further, these madnesses do not merely go on side by side; as they meet they mutually affect one another, and throw up each other's intensity ... this central Climax presents a terrible duet of madness, the wild ravings and mutual workings of two distinct strains of insanity, each answering and outbidding the other.[6]

Moulton seems almost to forget that Edgar's madness is feigned. But he continues:

When examined more closely this Centrepiece exhibits not a duet but a *trio of madness*; with the other two there mingles a third form of what may be called madness, the professional madness of the court fool.

To this we should add the near-madness of Gloucester ('I am almost mad myself') and the madness of the elements, a reflection in the macrocosm (the universe) of the madness of Lear himself. The various forms of madness together exemplify the break-up of society and the threat to the universe itself under the impact of ingratitude and treachery.

Heilman makes the point that the wicked characters, apparently entirely rational, are enslaved by their uncontrolled animal desire. Lear unconsciously hits off Gonerill and Regan when, in IV.6, he describes women as centaurs from the waist downwards, a mingling of crude materialistic rationalism with irrational lust. Regan and Gonerill are destroyed by their jealous rivalry, and Gonerill, who murders her sister, is prepared to murder her husband so that she can have Edmund to herself. Cornwall is killed by his servant because of his sadistic cruelty. Yet these evil characters think of themselves as governed by reason, and they use 'reason' to coerce others. The 'good wisdom' Gonerill recommends to her father is a demand for his capitulation; 'you ... should be wise' means, in effect, 'Dismiss your knights'; Albany's 'want of wisdom' is her way of describing his moral scruples. Heilman sums up the attitude of these materialists: 'Cool sanity is transmuted into moral madness.'

Another prominent theme is an enquiry into the nature of man, sometimes directly, as when in Act III Lear confronts Poor Tom, and sometimes indirectly, in the imagery concerned with animals and clothes. More than a century ago the first attempt was made to examine the animal imagery, when a critic counted 133 separate mentions of sixty-four different animals. Gonerill is compared with a kite, a wolf, a serpent and a monster. Gloucester in the blinding-scene compares himself with a baited bear, and Gonerill and Regan as wild beasts (III.7.55–63):

> Because I would not see thy cruel nails
> Pluck out his poor old eyes; nor thy fierce sister
> In his anointed flesh rash [= stick] boarish fangs ...
> If wolves had at thy gate howled that dern time,
> Thou shouldst have said, 'Good porter, turn the key ...'

In the storm-scenes Poor Tom uses animals (hog, fox, wolf, dog, lion) as symbols of the seven deadly sins. Albany, appalled by the treatment of Lear, tells Gonerill that if there is not divine intervention to punish such conduct, there will be a complete breakdown of civilization (IV.2.46–50):

> If that the heavens do not their visible spirits
> Send quickly down to tame these vile offences,
> It will come –
> Humanity must perforce prey on itself
> Like monsters of the deep.

The significance of the animal imagery is discussed by Heilman,[7] Wilson Knight,[8] W. H. Clemen,[9] and more succinctly by A. C. Bradley:[10]

As we read, the souls of all the beasts in turn seem to have entered the bodies of these mortals; horrible in their venom, savagery, lust, deceitfulness, sloth, cruelty, filthiness; miserable in their feebleness, nakedness, defencelessness, blindness.

Closely connected with the imagery which relates man to the other animals is that concerned with clothes and nakedness. The central symbol of this is Lear's attempt to strip off his 'lendings', his borrowing from the animals of furs, skins and wool. Earlier, in his reply to Regan's question: 'What need one?', he had urged her to 'reason not the need'; even the basest beggars possess things which, strictly speaking, are superfluous – Poor Tom has a blanket – whereas Regan's fashionably gorgeous garments scarcely keep her warm.

Poor Tom himself contrasts his present squalor, with only a blanket to cover his nakedness, with his former finery (in his invented past) when he was 'proud in heart and mind', curled his hair, wore gloves in his cap, and possessed three suits and six shirts. He warns against the rustling of silks because it leads to sexual temptation.

When Lear speaks of the 'poor naked wretches', it is not merely an expression of compassion; it is also (as Heilman argues) 'in the symbolic context, a recognition of the fate of the innocent in the world'. In his madness, Lear uses clothes as a symbol of class distinctions and of their effect on the way the law is administered: 'Thorough tattered clothes great vices do appear;/Robes and furred gowns hide all.' Even in our more democratic society a well-dressed defendant in a magistrates' court may well be treated more leniently than one less respectably attired.

In one of the Shakespearian scenes of *Pericles*, the hero, recovering from his melancholia on being reunited with his lost daughter, Marina, calls for fresh garments. So the fresh garments in which Lear is arrayed in IV.7 are a way of showing his return to sanity.

As Maurice Charney has said, clothes

represent the values of society, of the status quo, of an external socially conceived morality, whereas nakedness is the traditional image of unadorned truth; of innocent and vulnerable babes, fools and madmen, also of a wild and bestial nature, untempered by law, kindness, or justice.[11]

Caroline Spurgeon, in her pioneering study of Shakespeare's imagery, claimed that the dominant image of the play, the one most frequent in occurrence, was that of

a human body in anguished movement, tugged, wrenched, beaten, pierced, stung, scourged, dislocated, flayed, gashed, scalded, tortured and finally broken on the rack.[12]

Many of the best-known passages in the play contain images from this group. Lear, for example, declares that his frame of nature was wrenched from the fixed place, or thinks of himself as bound upon a wheel of fire, scalded by his own tears; and, as he dies, he is described as stretched on 'the rack of this tough world'. Shakespeare, however, was not merely concerned with the sufferings of the victims in the play (Lear, Gloucester, Edgar, Cordelia); he was universalizing the situation and implying that in the perspective of tragedy, necessarily one-sided and selective in its emphasis, this is the general fate of mankind. The suffering is more important than the cause. No answer is possible to Lear's last question: 'Why should a dog, a horse, a rat have life,/And thou no breath at all?'

The scriptural attempt to answer the question of life's unfairness is the book of Job. Job, an admittedly righteous man, is visited by a series of disasters—the loss of his livestock, the slaying of his servants, the accidental death of all his sons and daughters, and he himself smitten with boils. His three friends try to make him admit that he is being punished for his sins, but he refuses. In the end God speaks out of a whirlwind, rebuking Job's friends, but showing that it is impossible for man to understand God. Job is restored to prosperity and health, with the same number of sons and daughters as before and twice as many livestock. Most modern readers are left with the feeling that God's permission to Satan to tempt Job was scandalous, and that the final compensation does not excuse the way he has been treated. But the Geneva version of the Bible (used by Shakespeare) explains that

In this history is set before our eyes the example of a singular patience. For this holy man Job was not only extremely afflicted in outward things and in his body, but also in his mind and conscience, by the sharp tentation of his wife and chief friends

Shakespeare had Job in mind when he wrote some scenes of *King Lear*, as several critics have suggested. W. H. Gardner, for example, says that 'the stature and bearing of the sufferers [Job and Lear] give them a universal significance. The storm of *Lear* may be considered as much a symbol of divine intervention and judgement as the lightning and whirlwind which preceded the voice of God in *Job*.'[13] That Shakespeare was recalling the story of Job can be guessed from Lear's references to boils (II.4.218–20). Throughout the play we are reminded of man's suffering and the patience needed to endure it. Lear prays, 'Give me that patience, patience I need', and later he declares, 'I will be the pattern of all patience.' Kent asks him: 'Sir, where is the patience now/That you so oft have boasted to retain?' Edgar advises his father, 'Bear free and patient thoughts', and Lear tells him: 'Thou must be patient'. In Cordelia, grieving for her father, we are told, 'patience and sorrow strove'. Lear cries in the storm: 'I will endure'. 'Men must endure,' Edgar tells his father. And when Lear dies, Kent comments, 'The wonder is he hath endured so long.'

John Danby argued[14] that the patience advocated by characters in *King Lear* and exemplified by Cordelia is essentially Christian, rather than the stoicism of Seneca with which many critics have compared it. But although the distinction was doubtless clear to Elizabethan preachers, it is one difficult to make in the context of the pagan setting of the play. In any case, it is not denied that biblical teaching was reinforced both by classical philosophers and by humanist moralists. The union of pagan and Christian ideas can be found in Boethius, whose famous treatise on the consolations of philosophy had been translated in the reign of King Alfred and more recently by Elizabeth I. Shakespeare was presumably acquainted with Chaucer's intervening version.

It has been argued by Curtis Brown Watson that Lear's heroic efforts to maintain calm and dignity, his determination not to weep, during the first three acts are what makes him 'a tragic figure of the greatest stature ... weak and infirm he is, but, for the Renaissance moralists, magnanimity did not depend on bodily strength, but on greatness of soul, of mind, heart and will, which Lear manifests in abundance after his initial arrogance'.[15] Not merely his attempt to endure affliction patiently, but even his anger at his daughters' ingratitude and his desire for revenge 'would have met with a completely sympathetic response from the Jacobean audience', in whom Christian teaching and notions of honour were often at war.

This raises the question of the validity of J. C. Maxwell's description of *King Lear* (a description he afterwards retracted when I mentioned it to him), that it was a Christian play in a pagan setting. We have already seen that the source-play was given a Christian setting, despite the fact that the legendary Leir lived before the birth of Christ; and we have noted that Shakespeare eliminated all overt Christian references. The characters invoke Apollo, Juno, Jupiter and Nature, and they swear by the sun and by the mysteries of Hecate and the night. Yet it has often been recognized that there are a number of Biblical echoes, whether deliberate or accidental. When, for example, Cordelia claims that the invasion is not an act of aggression, but in support of her father: 'O dear father,/It is thy business that I go about', we are bound to be reminded of the reply of the boy Jesus when he was found by his parents in the temple: 'Wist you not that I must go about my Father's business?' Another example is furnished by the King of France's words about his bride: '... most rich, being poor,/

Most choice, forsaken, and most loved, despised'. As Hunter suggests, 'some of the resonance of these lines no doubt comes from the reminiscence of 2 Corinthians 6:10, where Paul speaks of the ministry of Christ as 'poor, yet making many rich, as having nothing, and yet possessing all things'.

A third example is more controversial. A gentleman declares that Lear has 'one daughter/Who redeems nature from the general curse/Which twain have brought her to'. The twain are, of course, Gonerill and Regan; but Carter, Danby and Hunter, to name no others, think that there is also an allusion to Adam and Eve and the Fall of Man, suggested by 'the general curse'. Most critics agree that there are references to Doomsday and that the predictions to which Gloucester refers are close to those in the gospels concerning the last days (see Matthew 24, Mark 13). Wittreich, moreover, points out[16] that the prophecy at the end of Malachi is often correlated with New Testament prophecies.

It is possible that Shakespeare, who was perforce a regular churchgoer, and who was familiar with at least two versions of the Bible (the Bishops and the Geneva) besides those passages included in the Anglican Prayer Book, was so steeped in scriptural phraseology that he used it without his audience or himself being aware of it. After all, there are echoes of the Bible in every one of his plays, as Richmond Noble demonstrated. Yet many critics have been convinced that *King Lear* is imbued with Christian ideas – especially if they are Christians themselves. W. R. Elton lists a number of these critics[17] – R. W. Chambers who calls the play 'a vast poem on the victory of true love', J. Dover Wilson who compares the death of Lear with Calvary, Geoffrey L. Bickersteth and John Danby who compare Cordelia with Christ, and many others. Elton's own eloquent chapter on Cordelia and Edgar shows that they belong to the category of virtuous pagans, and that Cordelia especially exhibits Christian virtues. She is associated with grace, love and benediction; her tears are holy water, her eyes heavenly, and she is a believer in providence and divine justice:

> Cordelia, anticipating the higher virtues of faith, hope, and charity, seems to approach the contemplative virtues of wisdom (*sapientia*), knowledge (*scientia*) and understanding (*intellectus*).

Robert Speaight argues that Edgar and Cordelia 'answer, for those who have ears, the tragic agnosticism of the play', and that Cordelia

> is the point of transition between Shakespearian tragedy and the theophany of the Shakespearian close [i.e. in the plays of the final period]. She is Nature redeemed

and remade; she is mercy and reconciliation; she is the pole around which all the movement of *King Lear* revolves.[18]

Elton's main purpose, however, is to refute the argument of those critics who believe that King Lear is essentially Christian. He believes that not merely does the play indicate 'the fallibility of pagan heavenly reliance', but that two of the play's crucial events, the blinding of Gloucester and Cordelia's hanging, are 'the wilful operations of an upside-down providence in an apparently deranged universe', which would suggest 'an implicit metaphysical "absurdity"'. Although Elton does not mention the Theatre of the Absurd, it is clear that he would not seriously object to putting *King Lear* in that category. He concludes that

> By depicting a superstitious pagan [Lear himself] progressing toward doubt of *his* gods, Shakespeare secured for the play the approbation of the less speculative devout, who saw in its direction the victory of the True Faith ... Moreover he obtained for it the interest of those more troubled and sophisticated auditors who were not to be stilled by pious assurances in the unsteady new world of the later Renaissance.[19]

Perhaps Elton's conclusion does not follow inevitably from the evidence he has collected with so much care and learning. Supposing that Shakespeare was indeed a secret agnostic, it is strange that this is the only play in which we have hints of it. The tragedies written immediately before *King Lear* – *Hamlet* and *Othello* – are Christian in tone and setting; yet Shakespeare, had he so wished, could have excluded religious feeling from the primitive Hamlet tale, and there was no need for him to stress the fact that Othello was baptized. In *Macbeth*, written probably soon after *King Lear*, he writes on damnation from a normal Christian viewpoint, with great stress on the saintliness of Duncan and Edward the Confessor. The comedies written about the time of *King Lear* – *Measure for Measure* and *All's Well That Ends Well* – are both more than nominally Christian, unlike their sources. Moreover, even in the pagan worlds of *Cymbeline* and *A Winter's Tale* every reader notices Christian undertones, and in the latter there is even an anachronistic reference to Judas.

It is true that Edgar's prayer for the success of Cordelia's forces and Albany's prayer for the safety of Lear and Cordelia are ignored by whatever gods may be; but there is no reason why pagan gods, whether false or imaginary, should answer prayers; and though many of Shakespeare's contemporaries believed in providential interventions, many others did not pretend that God was likely to protect the virtuous from the power of the wicked. The forces of Albany and Edmund were stronger than those of Cordelia; and it could be argued that Shakespeare, by showing that Lear and Cordelia could easily have been saved if Edmund had spoken a little sooner, was exploding naive ideas of prayer. Some contemporary theologians, Catholic as well as Protestant, were profoundly pessimistic about the possibility of happiness for the virtuous in this world. They believed that the good, who would be rewarded by an eternity of happiness in heaven, suffered their hell on earth.

It is essential to distinguish between the opinions of Shakespeare's characters, which may vary from scene to scene, and the meaning of the play, which is more than a synthesis of conflicting views. Nevertheless it is not unreasonable to suppose that sympathetic characters are more likely to express views of which the author approved, and which he expected the audience to share, than the evil characters. The evil characters in *King Lear* are all atheists.

Despite Lear's metaphor, or delusion, that he is bound upon a wheel of fire, tortured in hell, and his assumption that Cordelia is a soul in bliss, in heaven, there is no sign in the last scene that he, or anyone present, believes in an after-life. Lear's death is merely a release from the torture of life; Cordelia is 'dead as earth', her death being contrasted with the insignificant animals who are still living – dog, horse and rat. Although Lear's last words may indicate that he imagines he sees a movement of Cordelia's lips, this is plainly a delusion; and those critics who think that in this there is a kind of foretaste of the resurrection are, I believe, equally deluded. Such consolation would have negated the advantages of setting the play in a pagan world, before the advent of Christian hope. The sufferings of humanity were not to be compensated by an eternity of bliss, but merely alleviated by moments of reconciliation, forgiveness and love. Virtue is its own reward. To seek other reward is to put oneself in the company of Gonerill and Regan, whose professed love for Lear was calculating and hypocritical.

It has been suggested that a Christian tragedy is liable to turn into a morality play in which the sinners are damned and the virtuous rewarded. In *Hamlet* and *Othello* Shakespeare got round this difficulty in two different ways. Hamlet is torn between his promise to his father and his religious doubts on whether the killing of his uncle, however guilty, is the right course of action. Othello believes that he has damned himself by the murder of the innocent Desdemona, but he may be saved by this very belief. (He does not consider that even if she were guilty he would still be damned for her murder.) Macbeth is fully aware that he has sold his soul to the devil, but Shakespeare enables us to understand and to sympathize with the suffering hero. In *King Lear* he starts from the hypothesis, whatever his personal beliefs, that the gods are indifferent, or hostile, or inexplicable, or even a man-made fiction, and that there is no after-life in which the injustices of life on earth may be set right. It follows that human beings are entirely responsible for their actions, and that if these lead to disaster, the tragedy is absolute.

This is a perennial problem for theologians. In the book of Job, as we have seen, the apparent injustice was finally ascribed to the impossibility of understanding God. Isaiah declared (45:15): 'Verily thou art a God that hidest thyself'. Both Calvin and Luther thought that God was *absconditus* (hidden) and Montaigne too believed that God was incomprehensible. In his book on Pascal and Racine,[20] Lucien Goldmann quotes the Marxist critic Lukács to the effect that, in tragedy, God never intervenes 'either by word or deed in what the actors are doing' ... 'Man must live alone and by himself. The voice of the Judge has fallen silent for ever.' Goldmann doubts whether these ideas suit Shakespearian tragedy, and certainly they are not applicable to *Othello* or *Macbeth*. But Lear himself believes that God is hidden, when he accuses the gods of not taking his part, of allying themselves with Gonerill and Regan, of allowing Cordelia to die. Indeed, Elton thinks that when Lear seeks a natural cause of the thunder, or asks if there is a natural cause of hardness of heart, he is becoming sceptical about the existence of the gods. But when Lear takes Poor Tom for a professional sage, acquainted with the secrets of nature, he was not necessarily being sceptical. 'Whereof cometh the thunder?' was one of the questions in *Boccus and Sydrac*,[21] and according to Ovid,[22] Pythagoras considered 'whether Jove or else the winds in breaking clouds do thunder'. Natural causes do not rule out the existence of God, any more than Edgar's bogus miracle proves that all miracles are bogus.

The play as a whole may possibly leave us with the impression that the dramatist shares the opinion of his protagonist. Shakespeare seems to be saying to his audience: 'Let us assume for the purposes of this play, not for other plays, that the Christian belief in heaven and hell may be a delusion; that God, if God exists, is hidden and unknowable.' How should we then conduct our lives? On what principles should we try to organize society? What do men need? The answers implied in the play to these questions are not really in doubt. We need patience, love, forgiveness and the fruits of the spirit enumerated by St Paul, faith, hope and charity, the virtues advocated indeed by all the great religious teachers. In other words, the absence of heavenly rewards and hellish punishments should not affect our behaviour. Deprived of Christian hope, it has been said, we should still be bound by Christian ethic. For, in the last analysis, all of us would rather be Cordelia than her sisters, Edgar than Edmund, Albany than

Cornwall, Kent than Oswald, and we would not change our minds if the wicked, who are all destroyed, had triumphantly survived.

Robert Ornstein declared[23] that Shakespeare alone penetrates beneath archaic systems

to bring to light once more the indestructible certainties of the human spirit: its capacity for love, devotion and joy; its resources of courage and compassion in the face of unimaginable terror.

He went on to suggest that *King Lear*

actually celebrates the vulnerability of man, the sublime folly of his 'needs' and aspirations, the irrationality of his demands upon the vast inscrutable universe which surrounds him.

Maynard Mack makes a similar point[24] when he says that it is our capacity to suffer that gives us 'access to whatever grandeur we achieve'.

It will have become apparent from these and other comments that critics tend to discover in *King Lear* a reflection of their own philosophies of life. Professing Christians find in it nothing incompatible with their own beliefs, since the play is set in a pre-Christian world; agnostics regard it as a testament of agnosticism; existentialists can point to it as a central embodiment of their beliefs, since the whole emphasis is on individual responsibility. Yet almost all are united in their interpretation of what the play recommends concerning the rules which should govern human behaviour.

We have seen that the play raises questions of providence, and that it may prompt the suspicion, entertained by many people at some time in their lives, that success depends not on the practice of Christian virtues, but on their opposites – on pride, ambition, avarice, greed, lust, dishonesty, envy and competitiveness. The play continually stresses the corruption of the legal system, the abuses of authority, the hypocrisy of society and the immoral inequalities of the social system. We cannot evade these charges by shrugging them off as a madman's delusions, irrelevant to our more civilized age.

Nor, as we have seen, must we be driven to accept the view that the central meaning of the play, as expressed by a multiple murderer as the forces of retribution close in on him, is that life 'is a tale told by an idiot ... signifying nothing'. It is necessary to stress this point because some recent productions have been heavily influenced by Jan Kott's *Shakespeare Our Contemporary* (1964),[25] in which *King Lear* is treated as an absurdist play and compared with Samuel Beckett's *End Game*. A famous essay by G. Wilson Knight, 'Shakespeare and the Comedy of the Grotesque', has also been used to support the absurdist position. It is true that Knight speaks of 'the demonic laughter that echoes in the Lear universe', declares that 'the core of the play is an absurdity, an incongruity', and that Shakespeare walks 'the tight-rope of our pity over the depths of bathos and absurdity'. He illustrates these remarks by the Fool's derisive comments on his master's conduct, by ludicrous episodes in Lear's mad scenes, by the 'tragically absurd' attempted suicide of Gloucester, and by the murder of Cordelia:

> To be hanged, after the death of her enemies, in the midst of friends. It is the last hideous joke of destiny: this – and the fact that Lear is still alive, has recovered his sanity for this.

But we have to remember that Knight (as he confesses) was concentrating on one aspect of the play in order to bring out the grotesque element, and that his other essay on the play, also published in *The Wheel of Fire*, redresses the balance.

I may add that when Knight played Lear at Leeds in 1951, I noticed that he made certain that any laughter was not directed at him. The Fool acted as a laughter-conductor, so that Lear's dignity remained unscathed.

Another critic who stresses the comic element in *Lear* is Susan Snyder, who points out that

> *King Lear* is full of the structures, motifs, and devices of comedy. It has a double plot and a developed Fool; it is concerned, like many comedies, with the passing of power from old to young; two of its characters are disguised through most of the play, one of them in a series of *personae* that allow him to manipulate other characters; the protagonists are forced out from society into educative confrontations in a natural setting and then return to society again; and this process is accompanied by the traditional disorder of comedy – social hierarchies turned upside down, logic and even sanity violated. The plot disregards probability as flagrantly as any romantic comedy, from the love-test that sets it in motion to the conclusion of the Gloucester action in chivalric challenge, triumph of disguised hero over villain, deathbed repentance of villain.
>
> These constant appeals to the world of romantic comedy function in a complex way. They are often twisted to serve, and intensify, the immediate tragic effect. Yet they simultaneously allow for a long-range hope, based on the well-established assumptions of comedy, that all the confusion and pain is leading to a positive conclusion.[26]

It is true that earlier audiences who encountered the play for the first time, especially those who had seen the old play, may well have expected a happy outcome, and the end, when it came, would have been correspondingly devastating. But audiences now will still appreciate the contrast between what happens and what would normally be expected to happen.

Although *King Lear* raises all kinds of religious and philosophical questions, it is essentially, as everyone recognizes, a play about parents and children, the only one of Shakespeare's tragedies in which this is the central theme. There is a poem by Goethe which begins: 'An old man is always a King Lear'. By this he meant that the old expect their children to look after them in their declining years, at the same time as they regard them with apprehension as those who will step into their shoes. In real life it is usually the same children who represent a threat as well as a promise, but in *King Lear* the children are divided into good and bad, extremely good and extremely wicked. As befits a poetic drama, Shakespeare deliberately chooses extreme cases, so that we can be presented with the situation in its starkest form. It may be mentioned that Giuseppe Cocchiara, who collected many different versions of the Lear folktale from many different countries as F. D. Hoeniger showed in 'The Artist exploring the Primitive',[27] linked the tale to 'other stories of fathers and banished children, sometimes daughters, sometimes sons'. One version, from Corsica, 'dwells on the king's madness' and his daughter's care restores him to his reason. We do not know whether there was a similar English folktale. But Shakespeare makes use of the parabolic quality of such tales in the neat division, in both plots, of the children into good and bad.

Yet the play, though rooted in the primitive and set in a legendary past, is also a commentary on what was happening in the age when it was written. We have already seen that it is concerned with the problem of beggars. There are many other links with contemporary matters. Rosalie Colie has shown the various ways in which the play reflects the crisis of the aristocracy. She quotes Stone's description of the aristocratic code which was under threat:

... voluntary service to the State, generous hospitality, clear class distinction, social stability, tolerant indifference to the sins of the flesh, inequality of opportunity based on the accident of inheritance, arrogant self-confidence, a paternalist and patronizing attitude towards economic dependants and an acceptance of the grinding poverty of the lower classes as part of the natural order of things.

These values, Colie comments, are striking illuminations of the value-system of the play, whereas many of the events and attitudes in the play – the reduction of Lear's retinue, the stocking of Kent, the unscrupulousness of the bastard, the behaviour of Oswald, the realization by both Lear and Gloucester that they have taken too little care of the poor – illustrate the threats to the aristocratic code.

John Danby also believed[28] that Shakespeare was concerned with a crisis, but one much wider than that affecting the aristocracy. He contrasts the two concepts of nature to be found in the play, that expressed by the good characters, and that expressed by Edmund in his first soliloquy; one assuming a 'co-operative reasonable decency in man' and an attempt to harmonize conflicting claims, the other assuming, as Hobbes was later to do, that the condition of man 'is a condition of war of everyone against everyone', so that without an absolute ruler the life of man is 'solitary, poor, nasty, brutish, and short'. Now obviously there was plenty of cut-throat competition and Machiavellian policy in the Tudor period, and plenty of traditional decency and genuine religion in the seventeenth century, but Danby may well have been right to see Edmund as 'the careerist on the make, the New Man laying a mine under the crumbling walls ... of an ageing society that thinks it can disregard him'.

Of course the relevance of the play to society goes far beyond any meaning it may have had for its original audience. When Gregori Kozintsev was making his film, he discussed with Shostakovich the incidental music he required. When he received the 'Lament', he wrote:

> Here in the film, in the very place where the powers of hatred, the demonic element of tragedy had broken free and raged, this voice grew strong ... The cry of grief, bursting through the dumbness of the ages, through the deafness of time, must be heard. We made the film with the very purpose that it should be heard.[29]

The cry of grief was also the cry of outrage at injustice. In the film we were shown visually what Shakespeare brings out in the sufferings of Poor Tom, and in the prayers of Lear and Gloucester on their previous lack of care for poor naked wretches. Both realize the need for a fairer distribution of worldly goods. Gloucester, conventionally, addresses the heavens; Lear, unconventionally, prays to the poor naked wretches, and, by a very daring stroke, suggests that if men distributed wealth more fairly, it would show the heavens more just. It is as though he thought that the gods needed to learn from man.

Our responsibility for others is presented most vividly in the parable of the sheep and goats (Matthew 25). At the Last Judgment, the one test which divides the saved from the damned is concerned with our treatment of our fellow human beings: to treat them well or badly is equated with our treatment of God:

> Then shall he say unto them on the left hand, Depart from me, ye cursed, into everlasting fire, which is prepared for the devil and his angels. For I was an hungred, and ye gave me no meat; I thirsted, and ye gave me no drink; I was a stranger and ye took me not in unto you: I was naked, and ye clothed me not: sick, and in prison, and ye visited me not.

This parable was the inspiration of the Doomsday plays in the Mystery cycles. It was also featured in pictures of the Last Judgment: there was one in the Guild Chapel at Stratford-upon-Avon, which Shakespeare must have seen.[30] It was also the inspiration of the Lyke Wake Dirge:

> From Brig o' Dread when thou may'st pass,
>   – Every nighte and alle,
> To Purgatory fire thou com'st at last;
>   And Christe receive thy saule.
>
> If ever thou gavest meat or drink,
>   - Every nighte and alle,
> The fire sall never make thee shrink;
>   And Christe receive thy saule.
>
> If meat or drink thou ne'er gav'st nane,
>   – Every nighte and alle,
> The fire will burn thee to the bare bane;
>   And Christe receive thy saule.

When Lear enters with Cordelia's dead body, the three survivors wonder if the sight signals the end of the world:

KENT   Is this the promised end?
EDGAR   Or image of that horror?
ALBANY   Fall and cease!

Earlier in the play the mad king, a ruined piece of nature, had been compared with the dissolution of the world: 'This great world/Shall so wear out to nought' - a comparison made easy by the belief that the microcosm (man) was a tiny version of the macrocosm (the great world, or universe). Joseph Wittreich has suggested[31] that the references to Doomsday are an indication that Shakespeare shared his contemporaries' fascinated interest in the Apocalypse, a book on which King James himself had written, and that the play is concerned with prophecy, not in the sense of foretelling the future, but in the Old Testament sense of interpreting the present and the historical past in the light of divine revelation. It fulfils Auden's definition of parabolic art: to persuade people to unlearn hatred and to learn love.

Reading or seeing *King Lear* is, and should be, a harrowing as well as an uplifting experience. Keats, bracing himself to re-read the play, wrote of burning through 'the fierce dispute/Betwixt damnation and impassioned clay'.

In our own time, Harbage maintained[32] that the final scene commemo-rated humanity's long, agonized, and continuing struggle to be human. This larger meaning gives our tears the dignity of an act of ratification and gratitude: to these still figures we have pitied we owe the gift of feeling pity.

Holloway declared[33] that the play is a confrontation of

the seemingly limitless chaos and evil ... Its affirmation is as exalted, humane and life-affirming as affirmation can be, for it lies in a noble and unflinching steadiness, where flinching seems inevitable, in the insight of its creator.

L. C. Knights similarly regards the play as an affirmation in spite of everything.[34]

Washington Irving once praised 'the Bard' for gilding the harsh realities of life with innocent illusions. But if one hopes to obtain innocent illusions from literature in general, and from tragedy in particular, one would be foolish to come to *King Lear*, which is deliberately designed to strip us of such illusions, as all great drama must do.

Commentary

A Note on Locations

G. K. Hunter's edition in the New Penguin Shakespeare quite properly does not give the location of each scene. This is because in the unlocalized staging of the Elizabethan theatre attention is called to the location when, and only when, it is necessary, as, for example, in the storm-scenes of Act III, when it is made clear that we are in the open country, outside a hovel, in the castle, or in a farmhouse or other building nearby. On occasion the stage can represent two places at once. At II.2.171 Kent goes to sleep in the stocks; he is still there at II.4.1; but, in between, the fugitive Edgar has a twenty-one-line soliloquy. While he is speaking we forget the presence of Kent, and we are for the time being transported from Gloucester's castle – presumably the courtyard – to a place where Edgar is hiding. On the modern stage, by darkening the set and shining a spotlight on Edgar, the change of scene is facilitated; but on the Elizabethan stage, in broad daylight, Shakespeare relied on the convention that the place was established by the words alone, or by noises. The Folio stage direction at II.4.279 (*storm and tempest*) and at III.1.1 (*storm still*); the references to a hovel (III.2.61, 78), to a high-grown field (IV.4.7) and to a tree (V.2.1) are some of the indications in the text.

The most vivid piece of scene-painting, however, is Edgar's description of the cliff on which Gloucester thinks he stands (IV.6.11ff.), and when Edgar later in the scene speaks of burying Oswald in the sand, either we must suppose that he is keeping up the deception of his father or that the whole scene has taken place on or near the beach.

In most productions of the play on the modern stage, scenery or lighting are used to indicate where the action is supposed to be; but often these devices jar with the verbal indications in the text.

In spite of the dangers of getting bogged down in naturalism, it may be helpful, for a first reading only, to add a few notes on locations:

I.1   1–282   Lear's palace
       283–306   This dialogue would appropriately take place in a private room
I.2   Gloucester's castle
I.3   A room in Albany's palace

I.4	A hall in Albany's palace
I.5	A courtyard of Albany's palace
II.1	A courtyard of Gloucester's castle
II.2	The same
II.3	See note above
II.4	A courtyard of Gloucester's castle
III.1	The country near the castle
III.2	The same
III.3	A room in the castle
III.4	Outside the hovel
III.5	A room in the castle
III.6	A farmhouse or outbuildings near the castle (see III.4.146)
III.7	A room in the castle
IV.1	Near the castle
IV.2	Albany's residence
IV.3	The French camp at Dover
IV.4	Country near Dover
IV.5	Either Gloucester's castle (now Edmund's) or Regan's
IV.6	Near Dover, either in fields or on the beach
IV.7	A tent(?) in the French camp
V.1	In the British camp
V.2	Between the two armies
V.3	In the British camp.

Scene 1

[1–32] In accordance with Shakespeare's usual practice, the play opens not with the central character, but with others who prepare the way for his entrance (see, for example, the first scenes of *Hamlet, Macbeth, Timon of Athens, Antony and Cleopatra, Romeo and Juliet*). We are introduced to two of the three characters of the sub-plot (Gloucester and Edmund) and to Lear's most faithful servant, Kent. A great deal of information is packed into these thirty-two lines about Gloucester's character and about the king's intentions. We learn that Lear is about to abdicate and divide the kingdom. At first we understand that Albany and Cornwall are the two recipients. We do not hear that they are married to Gonerill and Regan. There is no mention of Cordelia. The surprise shown that Albany and Cornwall are to be given equal shares may alert us to the moral difference between the two men that soon becomes apparent.

It is often asserted that the division of the kingdom was implicitly condemned by Shakespeare, as he might have been expected to do at a time when James I, before whom the play was performed, was urging the union of England and Scotland. It has been pointed out that the political moral of *Gorboduc*, the earliest English tragedy, performed before Elizabeth I, was to urge her to beget an heir and so avoid the disastrous civil war between Gorboduc's sons as a result of his unwise abdication. With hindsight we can see that Lear's abdication was fraught with similar disaster, with civil war threatened as early as Act II. But as Lear was over eighty and had no male heir, it was natural and proper for him to settle the succession. Neither Kent nor Gloucester raises any objection to the division as such, as they could easily have done at this point in the play. Paradoxically, however, none of the virtuous characters ever accepts the reality of Lear's abdication and they regard him as king throughout. The ambivalence of Lear's role after the division of the kingdom is one of the mainsprings of the tragedy.

Gloucester reveals that Edmund is his illegitimate son. He describes the good sport he had had with the boy's mother only a short time after the birth of his legitimate son. He introduces Edmund to Kent, who comments on his fine appearance, and Gloucester then reveals that Edmund has been away in the country for nine years and will shortly be sent away again. Some critics believe that this sentence of banishment from court is the cause of Edmund's subsequent behaviour. Coleridge had another explanation: he thought that Edmund was outraged by the light way in which Gloucester had spoken of his mother. But we may note that Gloucester has fond memories of his love-affair and does not speak of his mistress as an evil woman, as the Paphlagonian king does. Moreover, Edmund later boasts of his bastardy. There is no evidence that he was compensating for feelings of shame.

Up to this point the scene, being introductory and conversational, has been in prose. With the entrance of Lear, the central character engaged on a ritual abdication, Shakespeare appropriately uses verse.

[33–282] It is apparent from the map, prepared beforehand, that the kingdom has been divided into three, and that Lear intends the best part of the kingdom to go to Cordelia, the daughter he loves best, the one with whom he hopes to live (85). The nature of the division is already known, the public ceremony merely confirming a previous decision. It is also clear that the love-test (which is an integral part of all versions of the Lear story, and features in other stories too) was, in Shakespeare's play alone, an afterthought on Lear's part. The king wants his three daughters to express their love and gratitude, a foolish, but not an unusual, wish. The plan misfires for several reasons. First, Lear is used to flattery (as he afterwards confesses) and this is a drug which, to be effective, has to be administered in ever-increasing doses. Secondly, Lear is an autocrat with absolute power, and his whim is law. Cordelia's refusal to take part in his autocratic charade undermines his authority, which leads him to reassert it through her banishment. Thirdly, Gonerill and Regan are aware of Cordelia's character and they know that she will not compete with them, if they exaggerate their affection sufficiently. Fourthly, Cordelia knows that her sisters are incapable of love, and she herself is unable to make use of her genuine love for material advantage. This is called pride by Lear, but it is surely a proper pride, which is a reflection of her integrity.

There will always be readers and spectators who become exasperated both with Lear and with Cordelia. Why is Lear unable to realize, as Kent and France do, that Cordelia actually loves him, while her sisters do not? Is it credible that he should have failed to realize over the years that two of his daughters were cold-hearted and self-seeking? These are questions likely to be raised by people familiar with modern naturalistic drama or with novels. Nevertheless, they miss the point. Shakespeare was dramatizing a fable, a kind of parable, with an obvious moral attached. It is the initial situation from which the tragedy springs: a man makes a fatal misjudgement, just as in the sub-plot another father believes his wicked son and disbelieves his good one. We should also remember that in the seventeenth century it was frequently said that hypocrisy was the one evil which even angels could not discover. There is a good example in *Paradise Lost*, when the angelic sentinel, detailed to guard Adam and Eve, obligingly directs the disguised Satan who asks the way to Eden.

A related misunderstanding is to imagine that if only Cordelia had been tactful, she would have humoured her father, and not understated, as she obviously does, her genuine love. The answer to this is provided by Kent, who, throughout the play, directs our responses; and by the King of France, who understands the nature of her reticence: '... a tardiness in nature/Which often leaves the history unspoke/That it intends to do', where speech and action are contrasted. France, like the audience, immediately appreciates Cordelia's value: '... most rich, being poor,/Most choice, forsaken, and most loved, despised'.

How materialistic her sisters are can be seen from the imagery they use to describe their 'love' for their father. Gonerill's stress on words of valuation – dearer, rich, rare – is echoed by Regan. Indeed, at this point in the play there is no apparent difference between their characters. They are almost personifications of hypocrisy, or what Shakespeare often called 'seeming'. He regarded it with particular loathing and, knowing that a good actor on the stage can assume a wide range of roles, he must have pondered on the difficulty of gauging sincerity.

Cordelia has fewer words to say than almost any other important character in Shakespeare's plays. This paucity of words is an index to her character, while her quiet, sad statement that she has 'nothing' to say is the first of many uses of the word. Her two asides, commenting on her sisters' speeches, are necessary so that the audience are left in no doubt of her motives. She cannot compete in the indecent auction. Her love is an end, not a means to an end other than love. She goes on to define her love in a way that would satisfy a reasonable father. She loves according to her bond, with the love and honour properly accorded to parents; but, on the brink of marriage, she cannot say she loves her father *all*. Like Desdemona, Othello's bride, she perceives a divided duty. (Many fathers more reasonable than Lear feel a pang when they realize they are no longer first in their daughters' affections.)

Lear's fury with the daughter he loves is caused by his bitter disappointment. It resembles the anger of a rejected lover. He had hoped to spend his last years with her – to set his 'rest/On her kind nursery'. The imagery also suggests a 'second childhood'.

His curse reveals for the first time that the play is set in a pagan world: he swears by the mysteries of Hecate (though Hecate also features in *Macbeth*), by Jupiter and by Apollo. We have already discussed (p. 11) why Shakespeare departed from the Christian setting of the old play – either because he knew that Lear reigned before the birth of Christ, or because he wished to give himself greater freedom in dealing with controversial religious issues. He was not entirely consistent, however, as we shall see in later scenes. In his great film, Gregori Kozintsev reconciled the play's pagan setting with the Christian undertones contained in the dialogue by assuming that Britain had lapsed into paganism, whereas France remained Christian. This was conveyed by having Cordelia married in a Latin ceremony as she embarked for France.

In abdicating, Lear emphasizes that he intends to retain the title of king and all the 'additions' – the honours, including a royal retinue. He does not realize, as the Fool is quick to point out, that when he gives up his power he inevitably puts himself in the power of others. He is utterly dependent on his favoured daughters and on the gratitude of their husbands. As we soon discover, Albany is the only one of the four with decent instincts, and he is at first dominated by the beautiful Gonerill.

Kent, the honest counsellor who offers unpalatably sound advice instead of the flattery to which the king is accustomed, is spurred into action by his outrage at the injustice to Cordelia, as well as by his own loyalty to Lear, whom he has loved, honoured and served. The love and honour of such a man show that Lear was not always as unjust and foolish as he now appears. Now, and later in disguise as Caius, Kent does not mince words. He calls the king mad, foolish, hideously rash, guilty of evil. His inevitable reward is banishment, ironically dispensed by a king in the process of abdicating authority, and he retorts that, as one cannot be free under a tyrant, he will continue a free man, a truth-teller, in a new country. His farewell speech, commending Cordelia to the gods and reminding Gonerill and Regan of their promises, is in rhymed couplets, the formality of which underlines their choric function. Kent speaks not merely in character, but as spokesman for the poet. Gloucester, another character who might have offered the king sound advice, is not present at either the love-test or Kent's banishment.

The reactions of the rivals for Cordelia's hand are nicely contrasted. Burgundy puts wealth and status above love; France, responding to Cordelia's obvious integrity, finds his love increased by her outcast state. His words have additional resonance because of their echoes of St Paul. France dismisses his rival with one scornful epithet ('waterish') in his praise of the dowerless Cordelia. The rhymed verse, like Kent's, has a choric function. So, too, does Cordelia's 'stood I within his grace,/I would prefer him to a better place'. And her final answer to Gonerill's sneer:

> Time shall unfold what plighted cunning hides;
> Who covers faults, at last with shame derides.

That truth is the daughter of time was a frequently used proverb, and it is here linked with a verse from the Old Testament (Proverbs 28:13), 'He that hideth his sins, shall not prosper.' (The chapter was appointed to be read on St Stephen's Day – the day on which *King Lear* was performed before James I – see p. 117.)

[283–306]   In the last section of this scene, for the conspiratorial dialogue between Gonerill and Regan, Shakespeare reverts to prose, which points a contrast with their inflated speeches to their father. This is what they really think. Gonerill emerges as the dominant character, Regan merely agreeing; and Regan's proposal to 'further think of it' contrasts with Gonerill's determined 'We must do something, and i' th' heat.' What they say about Lear is substantially true, but this does not excuse the tone of their remarks. Their total lack of filial affection prepares us for the horrors that follow.

The first scene of the play is virtually a prologue. We have been introduced to all the main characters except Edgar and the Fool. We have been warned of the probable results of Lear's foolishness in banishing Cordelia and Kent. But we do not yet suspect that Gloucester's adultery will also have dire results, for Edmund's character and ambition are not revealed until the beginning of the next scene.

Scene 2

Instead of continuing with the action expected from Gonerill's threats, Shakespeare interposes the parallel action of the sub-plot, in which another foolish father is deceived by his bastard son into believing that his virtuous and loving son wishes to murder him. All we know about Edmund from his brief appearance at the beginning of the play is that he is good-looking, polite and illegitimate. The soliloquy that opens the scene is something of a shock. In it Edmund boasts of his bastardy, closely following one of the paradoxes of Ortensio Lando (1543): 'That the Bastard is more worthy to be esteemed than he that is lawfully born or legitimate'. Anthony Munday promised to include this paradox in a volume which appears not to have survived,[1] but Elton lists more than a dozen references to similar eulogies of bastards.

Edmund is initially popular with audiences: he is clever, humorous, handsome and sexually attractive, while his virtuous brother appears to be an incredibly stupid dupe. Edmund is, moreover, an admirable actor, adopting different roles with father and brother, as he does later with Cornwall, Regan and Gonerill.

Nature, addressed by Edmund as a goddess, differs from the nature Lear later addresses as 'dear goddess'. John Danby made this difference the basis of his influential book, *Shakespeare's Doctrine of Nature*. In it he argued that the virtuous characters in the play look on nature as beneficent, whereas the evil characters regard nature as a mere justification for their unscrupulous pursuit of success. As Edmund declares in the last line of the scene, 'All with me's meet that I can fashion fit.' The end justifies the means.

The play has also been thought to dramatize the crisis of the aristocracy in Shakespeare's day. Yet it should be noted that whereas the new realists in the play are all atheists, this could not be said of the Parliamentarians who came to resist the power of the king and the court.

Edmund, as his soliloquy makes clear, is determined to rise in the world, and even his love-affairs are subordinated to his ambition. It is only when his ambition to be king is finally thwarted as he lies dying that he can attempt, however belatedly, to reprieve his last victims.

Perhaps in one respect Edmund arouses undeserved sympathy from a modern audience. He scoffs at his father's belief in astrology; and, although Gloucester is superstitious, some members of the original audience would have regarded Edmund's scepticism as dangerous. The eminently sensible Kent, in endeavouring to explain the moral gulf separating Cordelia from her sisters, declares that the stars govern our condition. It is generally Shakespeare's evil characters who deride the influence of the stars. In *Julius Caesar*, it is the envious Cassius, in his temptation of the nobler Brutus, who tells him that the fault is not in our stars, but in ourselves.

It should be mentioned, too, that although the prediction quoted by Gloucester is similar to several made in Shakespeare's day, it is also close to the prophecy of the end of the world in Mark 13, when 'the brother shall deliver the brother to death, and the father the son, and the children shall rise against their parents, and shall cause them to die ... the sun shall wax dark, and the moon shall not give her light'.

Edmund's manipulation of Gloucester and Edgar has an almost comic effect, because of the contrast between his cleverness and their foolishness. His pretended defence of Edgar to his father, and his solemn 'That's my fear' to Edgar's announcement 'Some villain hath done me wrong', arouse laughter.

Despite the fact that the source of the main plot is 'historical' and the source of the sub-plot is fictional, the sub-plot seems more contemporary, closer to Shakespeare's own time, than the main plot. It is therefore appropriate that the scene – except for Edmund's initial and concluding soliloquies – should be in prose. Yet it has links with the more obvious poetry of the previous scene. The proverbial 'Nothing will come of nothing' is faintly echoed in Gloucester's witticism, 'If it be nothing I shall not need spectacles', and this looks back and forward to the frequent imagery connected with sight. The view, imputed to Edgar, that sons should manage the revenue of aged fathers, echoes what actually happens in the main plot. Nor is the view wrong in itself. The eminently humane and judicious Montaigne remarked:

> It is mere injustice to see an old, crazed, sinew-shrunken and nigh dead father ... to enjoy so many goods as would suffice for the preferment and entertainment of many children, and in the meanwhile, for want of means, to suffer than to lose their best days and years ... a father overburdened with years ... ought willingly to distribute ... amongst those, to whom by natural decree they belong.

Guazzo goes further. After saying that fathers who retain their paternal jurisdiction for too long make their sons into malcontents, he suggests that 'such men were worthy to dwell amongst the Caspians, who when the father is arrived to the age of threescore and ten, kill him presently, and give him to beasts to eat.' However, the outcome of Lear's disastrous experiment shows how Shakespeare explores both sides of the controversy.

Scene 3

Gonerill's plan of action is revealed in this short scene – to fasten on every opportunity of quarrelling with Lear, so as to drive him to seek shelter with Regan, who will continue to humiliate him. Neither sister, at this point, wants to kill him; they merely want to extricate themselves from the agreement by which they would each have an unwelcome guest for half the year.

In some recent productions the knights have been transformed into drunken boors, so that Gonerill's complaints seem fully justified. But it is made clear in the present scene that we cannot trust any word she says. She is the aggressor and, as we can see from the next scene, Lear has (rather surprisingly) refrained from complaints.

Lear is hunting; and Shakespeare introduced this touch from one of the possible sources to show that the king was still a very active octogenarian.

For Oswald's character, see the chapter on Characterization. He is

Commentary: Act I

nicely described by Kent (II.2.13ff.), if with some comic exaggeration, and more soberly by Edgar as 'a serviceable villain' and pimp. But, as we shall see, Shakespeare allows him a kind of loyalty, his last thought being of the delivery of Gonerill's letter to Edmund.

Scene 4

This scene is the longest in the play and it will be convenient to divide it into four sections.

[1–94] *The hiring of Caius*. Kent, now disguised as Caius, has shaved off his beard ('razed my likeness') and altered his accent (even the virtuous characters are forced to engage in 'seeming' once the tragic chain of events begins), at least until the end of Act II. Lear has been hunting, as in Layamon's medieval poem *Brut*, and his repeated requests for his Fool and for his dinner display the impatience which would make him a difficult house-guest. But his interview of Kent, and his subsequent employment of him, show both men at their best – the employment of Service by Authority. This helps to restore our respect for the king – it is the first time we have seen him since his banishment of Cordelia. Moreover, he behaves with astonishing restraint: 'I have perceived a most faint neglect of late, which I have rather blamed as mine own jealous curiosity than as a very pretence and purpose of unkindness.' The Knight to whom these words are addressed is manifestly very different from the debauched retinue later described by Gonerill.

Oswald's deliberate insolence – the 'weary negligence' authorized by his mistress – would have seemed more dreadful then than now. His treatment by Kent earns Lear's approval and confirms his appointment.

[95–184] *The Fool's instruction*. The Fool at last enters. As he is never on stage with Cordelia it has been surmised that the same actor played both roles. Nevertheless as the part was played by Robert Armin, whose previous parts included Touchstone in *As You Like It* and Feste in *Twelfth Night* – his last song in that play is echoed in III.2 – and as he is not known to have played female parts, the theory is improbable. The Fool's unexplained absence in the last two acts needs no explanation. Fools always wander in and out of plays. For Lear to refer to the Fool in his last speech, when all his attention and ours should be concentrated on Cordelia, would be a dramatic mistake. Yet during Cordelia's long absence from the stage the Fool acts, as it were, as her representative, never letting Lear or the audience forget her.

61

Later in the play the Fool labours to outjest Lear's heart-struck injuries; but this is not the impression we get from the present scene. It seems rather that his resentment at Lear's treatment of Cordelia expresses itself in savage attacks – in songs, in doggerel rhymes, and in sarcasm – on the foolishness of his master. In this one scene he tells him a dozen times that he is a fool, and he will not let him forget his injustice to Cordelia. Between I.1.263–4, when Lear says he will never see her face again, and IV.7.46, when he thinks she is a spirit in heaven, he hardly mentions her. In the present scene (263) he contrasts her 'most small fault' with Gonerill's, and at I.5.24, in an aside, he admits that he has wronged her. But he tries not to think of her, and the Fool, either because of his love for Cordelia or, less probably, because he is afraid that repression may lead to madness, continually harps on the wrong that Lear has committed.

Hazlitt remarked that the contrast between Lear's anguish and the petrifying indifference of his daughters would be too painful

> but for the intervention of the Fool, whose well-timed levity comes in to break the continuity of feeling when it can no longer be borne, and to bring into play again the fibres of the heart just as they are growing rigid from overstrained excitement.

In spite of Keats's admiration for Hazlitt as a critic, he commented in the margin of *Characters of Shakespeare's Plays*:

> And is it really thus? Or as it has appeared to me? Does not the Fool by his very levity give a finishing touch to the pathos; making what without him would be within our heart-reach, nearly unfathomable.

As Keats later realized, Hazlitt was aware that the Fool carries the pathos to the highest pitch of which it is capable (see p. 23).

[185–318]   *Lear and Gonerill*. The confrontation between the king and his eldest daughter, expected since the end of the first scene, postponed by the interposition of the sub-plot and adumbrated by Gonerill's instructions to Oswald in Scene 3, is sparked off by Gonerill's attitude to the all-licensed Fool. It is Gonerill who makes the first mention of the Fool and of Lear's protection of him (I.3.1) and her first complaint to her father concerns the Fool (I.4.196). Lear, as autocratic as Gonerill, yet recognizes the freedom of the Fool to criticize. Many absolute monarchs used their Fools not merely for amusement but as reminders that they were human and fallible. That Gonerill cannot accept humour, or satire, or criticism is a sign of her incurable egotism.

The attack on the behaviour of Lear's knights is delivered in the accents of shocked respectability – as a Puritan pamphleteer might deplore the behaviour of rakish cavaliers or Malvolio complain of Sir Toby Belch. We are not given an objective account, but the knights we do see behave properly and speak sensibly, and Lear's claim that they are 'men of choice and rarest parts' is nearer the truth than Gonerill's description of 'Men so disordered, so deboshed and bold'.

Lear's first reactions to Gonerill's attack is to pretend she is not his daughter (214), then that he has lost his own identity (222–6), then again that he does not recognize Gonerill, or that she is a 'Degenerate bastard'. These, of course, are pretences. He is putting on an act as a means of expressing his horror and astonishment. He is not really deluded: the onset of madness comes later. But the very fact of entertaining such possibilities will eventually drive Lear towards madness.

We learn that the request to Lear 'A little to disquantity your train' is the thin end of the wedge. Lear finds that half his train has already been disbanded (291). (As a hundred knights are mentioned three times later in the scene (319, 321, 329) there appears to be some confusion in Lear's mind or carelessness on Shakespeare's part.) The numbers of followers Gonerill and Regan propose to allow him are progressively reduced – fifty, twenty-five, ten, five – till, at the end of Act II, Regan tells him he does not need one.

It should be remembered that in Shakespeare's day the size of a retinue, not merely of monarchs but of nobles, was thought to be of immense importance. The cutting-down of Lear's retinue would have been regarded as a deadly blow to his honour and status, particularly insulting when coming from his daughters.

Lear acknowledges that he has made a terrible blunder in his division of the kingdom, but he does not yet admit that he was wrong to banish Cordelia – that comes in the next scene. It is the ingratitude of the favoured children that horrifies him. In *Julius Caesar*, Antony described how the ingratitude of Brutus had quite vanquished his benefactor, and in the play nearest in date to *King Lear*, Timon is obsessed by the ingratitude of the Athenians to whom he has been so extravagantly generous. Even in the middle comedies, one of Amiens' songs refers to the winter's wind 'that does not bite so nigh/As man's ingratitude'; and Viola hates ingratitude more than any vice which 'inhabits our frail blood'.

Lear's curse of Gonerill, at first with sterility and, failing that, with a thankless child so that her motherhood proves to be a prolonged martyrdom, is terrifying. It has been suggested from the later reference to 'young bones' (II.4.158) that she is already pregnant; and some actresses apparently ascribe her later, more savage, treatment of Lear to her horror at the curse. This is to read between the lines, and there is no indication in the text that she is particularly affected by Lear's words, or that her attitude to him is altered by them.

Albany has entered in time to hear Gonerill called a 'Detested kite' and he stands amazed at the terrible curse on her and on their offspring. He does not know of the provocation Lear has suffered, and protests his innocence and ignorance. Lear promises to tell him (293) but fails to do so in the fourteen lines before his exit.

[319–45] *Albany's doubts about Gonerill*. Albany begins to worry about Gonerill's attitude to her father. She scornfully dismisses his scruples. To her, wisdom is equated with harsh realism, and mildness or compassion is 'harmful'. She accuses him in effect of being weak and effeminate, and because he ignores Lear's threat to resume the throne, a danger as well.

Gonerill's humiliating treatment of her husband is underlined by her calling for Oswald and sending him on a confidential mission to Regan.

Albany is absent from the stage throughout the whole of the next two acts. We hear of disagreements of an unspecified kind between Albany and Cornwall, but these are presumably territorial disputes. Our interest is concentrated on Lear's madness and the betrayal of Gloucester, and when we next meet Albany (IV.2) he knows that Gonerill and Regan have driven their father mad, and soon afterwards that Gloucester has been blinded. He escapes from his subservience to Gonerill through his realization that she is evil.

Scene 5

Lear, waiting impatiently for horses to convey him to Regan, sends Caius ahead to announce his arrival. He does not know – and nor do we until II.1.58 – that Regan and Cornwall are about to visit Gloucester's castle. Editors assume (hopefully) that Lear is referring to the town of Gloucester, where Cornwall supposedly resides, but audiences surely are likely to assume that the earl is meant. Shakespeare, in fusing the two plots so that Gloucester's fate is linked with Lear's, found it dramatically necessary to have the success of Edmund's plot against Edgar, and the final humiliation of Lear by Gonerill and Regan, take place at Gloucester's castle. We are not told exactly where Cornwall resides, but as he is Gloucester's overlord, his 'arch and patron', it was presumably not far from Gloucester's castle. Having had Gonerill's letter, Cornwall and Regan arrive after a night's journey. By being away from home, they have an excuse for not receiving Lear before the expiration of the month he was supposed to be at Gonerill's.

The Fool continues to expose Lear's folly. He sees clearly that Regan will behave in exactly the same way as Gonerill. Lear himself has three remarks which could be marked as asides: his confession that he has wronged Cordelia (24); his fear of madness, here first expressed (43); and, between these, 'To take't again perforce' (37). Hunter, following Johnson, takes this to mean that Lear is thinking of resuming his power as a ruler (cf. I.4.306). But, in view of his next words – 'Monster ingratitude!' – Steevens's interpretation is more likely: he is thinking of Gonerill's ingratitude 'in taking away the privileges she had agreed to grant him' (i.e. the reservation of a hundred knights).

Act II

The action moves to Gloucester's castle, to which Regan and Cornwall have gone in order to avoid giving hospitality to Lear.

Scene 1

Curran, although given a name, does not appear again. He brings two pieces of news: that Cornwall and Regan are arriving that night, and that there is likely to be a war between Cornwall and Albany. This war never comes to anything, but it is referred to several times. Its causes are unspecified, but we may suppose it is a power struggle between the two dukes. In spite of Lear's avowed aim to avert future strife by dividing the kingdom in his lifetime, strife has not been prevented. The threat of conflict also serves to distance Albany from Cornwall – we might otherwise lump them together. Edmund, with characteristic agility, makes use of both pieces of news. He asks Edgar if he has not spoken against Cornwall and then, before he has had time to obtain an answer, if he has spoken against Albany. His mock fight with Edgar does not merely earn him the gratitude of his father, but also brings him to the attention of Cornwall and Regan. This is why he is delighted to hear of their approach.

When Gloucester appears on the scene, Edmund uses delaying tactics. He wants to give Edgar time to escape, as an immediate confrontation of Edgar with his father might ruin his plot. So he first speaks of Edgar's 'Mumbling of wicked charms', because he knows that suspicion of witchcraft will inhibit coherent thought in the superstitious Gloucester. Then he pretends that his self-inflicted wound is more serious than it really is. Finally in two long speeches he establishes his own moral credentials by his efforts to dissuade Edgar from parricide. He declares that when he threatened to expose the villainy of his brother, Edgar boasted that no one would believe the word of an 'unpossessing bastard' against his own denial. All this convinces Gloucester of Edmund's virtue and loyalty; and, taking a hint from the word 'unpossessing', he promises to make him his heir.

Gloucester and Edgar are both gullible, of course; but it is important to realize not merely that the noblest people are most credulous, but also that there was a well-established stage convention that the calumniator was always believed, and, beyond that, a belief that hypocrisy was impenetrable. In *Much Ado About Nothing*, it is not only the foolish Claudio who is deceived by Don John, but the sensible Don Pedro, and even Hero's father; and it is not only Othello who is hoodwinked by Iago, but Roderigo, Cassio, and his own wife, Emilia.

Edmund's skill in pursuing his ambitions is again illustrated when Regan asks if Edgar was a companion of Lear's riotous knights. Gloucester has no knowledge of this and does not see the point of Regan's question; but Edmund immediately realizes what she wants to hear, and says that Edgar was of that consort. (The word 'consort' has offensive associations, as we can see from the exchange between Mercutio and Tybalt in *Romeo and Juliet*.)

It is apparent in this scene that Regan dominates Cornwall, as Gonerill at first dominates Albany. She takes the initiative (102), or interrupts her husband (118), although he is said to be 'fiery' and obstinate. Edmund is enlisted by Cornwall, because, if there is going to be a war, he will need reliable soldiers, 'Natures of deep trust'. In view of Edmund's complete untrustworthiness, the irony is apparent. It is a case of evil gravitating to evil.

Scene 2

Kent, as we learn from his later account to Lear (II.4.26ff.), had arrived at Cornwall's house just before Oswald's arrival with letters from Gonerill to Regan, warning her of Lear's behaviour. It is clear that despite the threatened war between Albany and Cornwall, their wives are still allies in their plot against Lear. Both messengers were instructed to follow Cornwall and Regan to Gloucester's castle. Kent's previous dislike of Oswald would be increased by this episode. His splendid invective and Oswald's cowardice provide some rare comic relief. But Kent's belligerence, which lends colour to the accusations levied against the 'riotous knights' (although he is not a knight, but a servant), does not help his master's cause.

When the brawl is interrupted, Kent, half-forgetting his menial status, goes out of his way to be uncivil to Cornwall, first by insinuating that he loves flatterers and that Oswald is a pandar (70–77), then by the open rudeness of

> I have seen better faces in my time
> Than stands on any shoulder that I see
> Before me at this instant . . .

and by his parody of an affected flatterer (103–6). Immediately afterwards he drops into prose, so as to give the maximum contrast with the preceding inflated style. Cornwall points out that a pretence of plain-speaking can be a screen for something much worse. Shakespeare had made the same point in *Othello*, where Iago's plain-speaking, which wins him a reputation for honesty, is a cloak for villainy.

The lines 'None of these rogues and cowards/ But Ajax is their fool' refer to the situation in *Troilus and Cressida*, where the rogue and coward, Thersites, treats the valiant but unintelligent Ajax as a fool.

It has been pointed out that the stocks were used as the proper punishment for those who 'do unseemly behave themselves towards their betters', as Kent had obviously done. Yet to treat a king's messenger in this way, if not worse than murder, as Lear alleges (II.4.22), is certainly an outrage, as Gloucester at once realizes. Once again it is the virtuous characters who recognize the king's legitimate rights. Despite his subordinate relationship to Cornwall, his patron, he tries to intervene on behalf of the king's servant and he confesses that 'the Duke's to blame'. During the rest of the act Gloucester makes ineffectual attempts to mediate between Lear and his daughters. He is shattered by Edgar's supposed attempt on his life, and this adds to his ineffectiveness. In the end, however reluctantly, he consents to bar his doors against the king. Then in Act III he has second thoughts and comes down from the fence, fully aware of the risk he was running. Weak and vacillating as he is, Gloucester at last acts according to his conscience (see p. 80).

Kent's soliloquy in the stocks (158–71) is obscure in some of its details, either because of a faulty text or because he is reading disconnected snatches from the letter; but the general sense is plain enough. Cordelia has been informed of his disguise, and the letter tells him that she is 'seeking to give/Losses their remedies', i.e. to intervene somehow to protect Lear from her sisters. As Caius has been in the king's service for not much more than a day and Cordelia has not really had time to hear of Gonerill's treatment of her father, the time-scheme is deliberately left vague. It is not until the beginning of Act III that we learn of the French invasion, and the lines mentioning the matter were omitted from the Folio text (see p. 78). The audience gets the impression that Cordelia is planning to come to the rescue of Lear, but it will probably not have time during a performance to question the sequence of events.

Scene 3

While Kent is in the stocks, Edgar appears as a fugitive, who must 'other accents borrow'. He is obviously not in the courtyard of the castle, where the stocks are; but there is no reason to put the stocks in a recess or conceal them behind a curtain. An Elizabethan audience would be perfectly capable of ignoring the presence of Kent while Edgar is speaking. On the modern stage the usual method is to shine a spotlight on Edgar and leave the rest of the stage in darkness.

It will be recalled that Leonatus, the legitimate and good son of the Paphlagonian king, enlists as a common soldier. Shakespeare's alteration, of having Edgar disguise himself as a Bedlam beggar, 'the basest and most poorest shape', had various advantages. It enabled Edgar to appear in almost every scene, and as he was to encounter his father it was necessary for him to have an impenetrable disguise. Then, since Shakespeare wanted to reveal the minimum of man, what Lear called 'unaccommodated man', he needed to have a figure at the very bottom of the social scale; and this would give him the opportunity to probe what was a major social problem. Historians such as R. H. Tawney have written on the agrarian problem in the sixteenth century; and Karl Polanyi has described in *Origins of Our Time* (p. 43) the effects of the enclosure of common lands:

They were literally robbing the poor of their share in the common, tearing down the houses which, by the hitherto unbreakable force of custom, the poor had long regarded as theirs and their heirs'. The fabric of society was being disrupted; desolate villages and the ruins of human dwellings testified to the fierceness with which the revolution raged, endangering the defences of the country, wasting its towns, decimating its population, turning its overburdened soil into dust, harassing its people and turning them from decent husbandmen into a mob of beggars and thieves.

Shakespeare also required a feigned madness to contrast with the real madness of Lear. For this he plundered Samuel Harsnet's *Declaration of Egregious Popishe Impostures*, with its vivid and unpleasant accounts of counterfeit demoniacs and bogus exorcisms. The idea of feigned madness may have been prompted by the common knowledge that some of the Bedlam beggars were confidence tricksters. Dekker's description, in *The*

Bel-Man of London, of 'An Abraham Man' was written after *King Lear*, but he was describing a common type:

> Of all the mad rascals ... the abraham-man is the most phantastick: The fellow that sat half naked (at table to-day) from the girdle upward, is the best Abraham-man that ever came to my house and the notablest villain. He swears he hath been in bedlam, and will talk frantickly of purpose; you see pins stuck in sundry places of his naked flesh, especially in his arms, which pain he gladly puts himself to (being indeed no torment at all, his skin is either so dead, with some foul disease, or so hardened with weather) only to make you believe he is out of his wits. He calls himself by the name of Poor Tom, and coming near anybody cries out, Poor Tom is a-cold.

Shakespeare, unperturbed by the anachronism, has thrust a contemporary problem into the legendary period of the Lear story.

Edgar, as we have seen, begins as absurdly credulous (and see p. 59); at the end of the play he is the nominated king, and the audience must be willing to accept that he has, by that time, become credibly royal. To convince us that the one character has developed into the other is perhaps the hardest task Shakespeare set himself. Some critics, indeed, have thought that the poet was not wholly successful, either because Edgar's function as a commentator on the action conflicts with the reality of the character, or else because, as Leo Kirschbaum put it,[2] 'Edgar is not a mimetic unity; he is a dramatic device ... his various roles do not tell us more about Edgar. They tell us more about the play in which he is a character.' Kirschbaum was greatly influenced by two earlier critics, Edgar Elmer Stoll, and L. L. Schücking whose *Character Problems in Shakespeare's Plays* (1922) is an attempt to show that many of his characters are psychologically inconsistent because they are allowed to make what are virtually authorial comments on the action. Nevertheless I do not believe that the moralizing comments made by Edgar can be wholly equated with Shakespeare's views. He takes the place of the absent Fool in the second half of the play, and his remarks are the natural expression of the terrible experiences to which he has been exposed; and, since he is abnormally sensitive he experiences other people's anguish as well as his own. He declares truly that by 'the art of known and feeling sorrows', he is 'pregnant to good pity'. I believe, too, that the various roles he plays are the means by which he matures into royalty. He experiences first the withdrawal of his father's love and the treachery of his brother, which he is too unsuspicious to suspect. Then he feels the terror of a hunted outlaw. He disguises himself as a reject of society and, as Poor Tom, he assumes the additional role of demoniac. He suffers acutely from the sight of the king's madness, and again from his father's blinding. He saves his father from suicide by a bogus miracle, pretends to be another man at the foot of the cliff, adopts a more rustic dialect in his encounter with Oswald, and finally emerges as a chivalric champion who defeats his treacherous brother. He is not a man born to be king, but one who is trained by suffering to be worthy of the office.

Scene 4

In this scene, Lear is stripped of his last illusions about his favoured daughters. The hope that Regan would be kind and grateful is soon shattered. Emrys Jones claims[3] that the second act of the play 'is undoubtedly one of the grandest pieces of continuous dramatic writing in the whole of Shakespeare'. And on this particular scene he mentions

> its increasingly tight control, which in the final phase becomes focussed in the consciousness of the audience through the use of numbers ... As it develops the scene acquires a frightening ritualistic deliberateness, as if Lear were being ceremoniously baited, plucked of his feathers, stripped, ostracized. And as always in this kind of prolonged set scene, the action acquires rhythm through the use of repeated phrases, so that we move through several carefully gradated series, each of which has its precise quasi-musical rigour and, in performance, considerable power to agitate.

Seeing his messenger in the stocks, the refusal of Cornwall and Regan to speak with him, Regan's demand that he should return to Gonerill and ask her forgiveness, and the friendly greeting between the two sisters – these are a series of shocks which make Lear realize that the Fool's warnings had been fully justified. Thereafter the daughters reduce his hundred knights step by step to fifty, to twenty-five, to ten, to five, and finally to none at all. (Later Lear will voluntarily strip away not only his retinue but all superfluities in an effort to reach essential man.) The effect on Lear is cumulative. At first he is incredulous, refusing to believe Kent – the bandying of oaths (13–21) was altered in the Folio text (see p. 115), and the two versions of this passage should not be conflated – and he declares that Cornwall and Regan

> ... durst not do't;
> They could not, would not do't; 'tis worse than murder
> To do upon respect such violent outrage.

Kent gives an accurate account of the incident that led to him being put in the stocks, but he fails to mention that he had insulted Cornwall and Regan. Indeed he expressly denies that he had given any more offence.

Lear has an attack of *hysterica passio*. The standard work on the subject,

A Brief Discourse of a Disease called the Suffocation of the Mother by Edward Jordan, appeared in 1605, perhaps in time for Shakespeare to have read it; but the symptoms were well known. The disease, moreover, is mentioned more than once in Harsnet's tract and Michael Drayton describes the symptoms in a simile in *Polyolbion* (VII.19), in which a woman 'Starts, tosses, tumbles, strikes, turns, touses, spurns and sprawls,/Casting with furious limbs her holders to the walls.' But this appears to be a fit, quite different from Lear's sense of choking. Jordan, indeed, mentions that 'the principal parts of the body . . . do suffer diversely according to the diversity of the causes and diseases wherewith the matrix is offended'.

Up to this point the Fool's shafts have been directed against Lear's foolishness; now he broadens his target to embrace the ineradicable selfishness of humanity. Children are kind to their parents, he suggests, only in hope of gain. The poor are always badly treated by Fortune. When Kent asks why the king travels with so small a retinue, the Fool tells him he deserves to be put in the stocks for asking so naive a question, as earlier he had been offered a fool's coxcomb 'for taking one's part that's out of favour'. The king's followers are deserting him because his fortunes are declining. Kent is advised to follow their example:

. . . Let go thy hold when a great wheel runs down a hill, lest it break thy neck with following. But the great one that goes upward, let him draw thee after. When a wise man gives thee better counsel, give me mine again . . .

The wise man is the one who 'serves and seeks for gain', one who will desert his master as soon as he declines in wealth or power. But the Fool himself will not follow his own advice: he will tarry, and he hopes that only knaves will follow his advice. Enobarbus, who deserts Antony, nevertheless knows that

> . . . he that can endure
> To follow with allegiance a fall'n lord
> Does conquer him that did his master conquer,
> And earns a place i'th' story.

As in Erasmus's *Praise of Folly*, it is the worldly-wise who are spiritually foolish, the fools who are ultimately wise, a key concept in Pauline theology (see p. 99). In the first scene of *Timon of Athens*, written just before or just after *King Lear*, the Poet outlines his allegory of Fortune throned on a hill. It is intended as a warning to Timon that if he were to lose his wealth, if Fortune spurned him, all his dependants would 'let him slip down,/Not one accompanying his declining foot'. The prophecy is not entirely borne out by events. Although his flatterers all desert Timon when he becomes bankrupt, his servants all remain loyal. His steward, Flavius, speaks for all of them when they take a sorrowful farewell. They still wear Timon's livery. So in *King Lear* the Fool is unduly pessimistic: not merely do he and Kent remain faithful; but Gloucester, at the risk of his life, rallies to the king, and 'thirty-five or thirty-six' of his knights – not a bad percentage – convey him to Dover.

When Lear returns with Gloucester (84) he is convinced that the reasons given for not receiving him are mere excuses; and he is furious with the well-meaning Gloucester for confessing his powerlessness in the situation because of the 'fiery quality' of Cornwall: 'Fiery? The "fiery" Duke? Tell the hot Duke that –' Here Lear checks himself and, though near breaking-point, with surprising self-control admits that Cornwall may indeed be ill. Then, noticing Kent in the stocks, he again becomes convinced that illness is just an excuse. His threat to beat the drum succeeds in forcing Cornwall and Regan to appear. Regan pretends she is glad to see him; and Lear at first restrains his anger, but it is only just beneath the surface:

> If thou should'st not be glad,
> I would divorce me from thy mother's tomb
> Sepulchring an adult'ress.

Obviously he does not trust her, but he postpones raising the question of Kent's punishment, and addresses her as 'Beloved Regan'. Her defence of Gonerill and her suggestion that Lear is senile, that he should accept orders from more sensible people, and that he should return to Gonerill, are nicely calculated to infuriate him. But his fury is still directed against Gonerill. His only reply to Regan's accusation of senility is to admit, perhaps sarcastically, that all the old can expect is charity:

> Dear daughter, I confess that I am old;
> Age is unnecessary; on my knees I beg
> That you'll vouchsafe me raiment, bed, and food.

He curses Gonerill again in language as vehement as that of his original outburst (see p. 56), and so provokes Regan to make her sole reference to the gods: 'O the blest gods!/So will you wish on me when the rash mood is on.'

Whereas Gonerill is unmoved by her father's curses, Regan appears to be apprehensive. Lear is still hoping against hope that Regan will prove to be fundamentally different from Gonerill, but the speech which begins

> No, Regan, thou shalt never have my curse.
> Thy tender-hefted nature shall not give
> Thee o'er to harshness. Her eyes are fierce; but thine
> Do comfort, and not burn

becomes increasingly desperate; and when Regan says 'Good sir, to the purpose', he comes out with the question that has been nagging at him throughout the scene: 'Who put my man i' the stocks?', although he still has a faint hope that Regan did not know of it.

At this point Gonerill arrives and Lear appeals to the gods, who should love old men because they themselves are old, to take his side in the conflict with his daughters. Then, to his horror, he sees Regan take Gonerill by the hand – a proof that Regan agrees with what Gonerill has done. Lear again demands to know who put his man in the stocks, and this time he gets an answer from Cornwall. He can only say, feebly or sarcastically, 'You? Did you?'

The attacks by Gonerill and Regan are carefully orchestrated. They are both determined to go back on their agreement with him about his 'additions' and his knights, and they intend to reduce him to impotence, especially as he has threatened to reassume his regal powers. They have not yet planned to kill him. In spite of their cruel behaviour, they can still adopt a moralizing tone. Gonerill, the future adulteress and poisoner, professes to be shocked by the conduct of the knights; and Regan, the sadist, argues that Lear should apologize to Gonerill, and quite plausibly, since she is staying at Gloucester's, advances difficulties of housekeeping. They both accuse Lear of senility or 'dotage' – Gonerill uses the word three times – and when, at the end of the scene, Lear rushes out into the storm, they decide that the wise course is to shut him out. So Lear's deliberate exaggeration – '... oppose the bolt/Against my coming in' – becomes a self-fulfilling prophecy.

Some members of modern audiences, and some readers, who have experienced the difficulties of looking after aged parents or who have put them in geriatric wards, have sometimes expressed a sneaking sympathy for Gonerill and Regan at this point in the play. Shakespeare always gives the devil his due. Lear has behaved foolishly, he still clings to the power he has ostensibly renounced, and he is doubtless a difficult guest. Yet Shakespeare makes it clear that the cold-hearted calculators are evil, not just potentially evil, and that Lear is right to be outraged by their conduct. Before the end of this scene, all our sympathies are with him.

Regan's proposal that Lear should return to Gonerill, with fifty knights dismissed, he greets with a series of rising impossibilities. The idea that he should 'abjure all roofs' and live in the wilds is a choice to which he is driven before the end of the scene. That he should kneel to the King of France (whom he resents because his marriage to Cordelia was an implied criticism of his own conduct) is even more impossible – but he does kneel to the Queen of France. That he should act as a slave to the detested and detestable Oswald is the ultimate impossibility.

In his next speech, Lear, afraid of going mad, makes a magnificent attempt to control his anger. He thinks that by not seeing Gonerill in the future, he will be able to keep his resentment within bounds; but it breaks out in the accusation that she is a disease in his flesh, 'a boil,/A plague-sore, or embossed carbuncle/In my corrupted blood'. Immediately after chiding her in such terms, he adds, 'But I'll not chide thee.' He assumes optimistically that the time is bound to come when she will be ashamed of her behaviour. He will not ask Jupiter to destroy her with a thunderbolt, or report her conduct to him, as though the god were unaware of what was going on in his universe and required spies to inform him (cf. V.3.17). Lear is still under the illusion that he can keep his hundred knights and stay with Regan. She soon disillusions him on this point. It is not yet her turn to receive him; fifty followers is ample for his needs, nay, too many – twenty-five is all she will allow. Lear reminds her that he has given her and Gonerill all, and that they are breaking the conditions attached to the gift. Then he decides that as Gonerill's fifty is double twenty-five, her love must be twice Regan's. He is still suffering from the delusion, under which he suffered in the first scene of the play, that love is a commodity which can be quantified. In three lines Gonerill reduces twenty-five to five, and Regan reduces five to nil – 'What need one?'

Lear's reply, 'O, reason not the need!', is one of the key speeches of the play, touching as it does on several prominent themes. (See p. 15.) He argues that need is relative. Even those at the bottom of the social pyramid, 'Our basest beggars', possess things which are not strictly necessary. But Lear has occasion to revise this view when he encounters Poor Tom, who seems to have no superfluities, unless his blanket be so accounted. 'Superfluous' is a word used later both by Lear and Gloucester to mark the great divide between riches and poverty, the superfluities of the rich being enough to eliminate degrading poverty. This is the argument of the mutinous citizens in *Coriolanus*, who complain that the patricians refuse to share their superfluous corn.

We have seen (p. 39) that the imagery of clothing is one means by which Shakespeare exemplifies the gulf between what Disraeli called the two nations, the rich and the poor, and between the different sorts of justice the two nations can expect. The poor, as Lear points out, need clothes merely for protection against the cold, whereas Regan's fashionable and flimsy clothes scarcely keep her warm. They are needed for vanity, for status, and to attract men, such as Edmund. Clothing imagery, as we have seen, is regarded by some critics as the most important image-group in the play.

In the middle of the speech, when Lear is speaking of true need, he breaks off: he realizes that his own true need is patience, and this is emphasized by the repetition of the word. Patience, as we have seen, was thought to be the lesson taught by the book of Job; and this book may have been put into Shakespeare's mind by the boil to which he had compared Gonerill (218), for Job was notoriously afflicted with boils, or by the storm which is about to burst.

In spite of the prayer for patience, Lear immediately afterwards prays to the gods for the exact opposite: '... fool me not so much/To bear it tamely; touch me with noble anger'. He vows to have such revenges on the unnatural hags, his daughters, that the world will be amazed; but the next lines reveal that it is an empty threat: he has resigned his power and is impotent:

> I will do such things –
> What they are yet I know not; but they shall be
> The terrors of the earth.

The noise of the thunder may be taken to be Jupiter's, the Thunderer's, answer to Lear's appeal, or the breaking of his heart into a hundred thousand fragments, as he fears the onset of insanity, as he confesses: 'O Fool, I shall go mad!' The storm acts as an accompaniment to the madness into which Lear is now plunging. It has been said that when he looks into Regan's heart his wits begin to turn. One of the problems which exercise him during the storm-scenes is whether there is any cause in nature that makes these hard hearts, why Gonerill and Regan are so depraved – the mystery of iniquity.

The departure of Lear into the storm is followed by self-justification from Regan and Gonerill: they couldn't possibly accommodate 'the old man and's people' in Gloucester's castle; it is really Lear's own fault for being so foolish and obstinate; she would gladly receive Lear if he would come alone. They are not sorry for the stand they have taken, but they seem to realize that they might be criticized for it.

When Gloucester returns, Cornwall, Gonerill and Regan unite to browbeat him into acquiescence. Gloucester reminds them of the lack of shelter in the neighbourhood: 'For many miles about/There's scarce a bush.' Regan, moral to the last, declares that Lear's exposure to the elements will teach him a much-needed lesson:

> O sir, to wilful men
> The injuries that they themselves procure
> Must be their schoolmasters.

Since 'He is attended with a desperate train', the only wise course is to lock him out. The command is reinforced by Cornwall. Gloucester reluctantly obeys.

At this point in the play evil seems to be triumphant. Edmund has succeeded in his plot, and so have Gonerill and Regan in theirs. Lear's one loving daughter is exiled; Gloucester's loving son is a hunted fugitive; Kent has defied his sentence of banishment, but remains in disguise; the good intentions of Albany and Gloucester are treated with contempt; and Lear, Kent and the Fool are driven into the storm. But in the next act worse is to come: the madness of Lear and the plot against his life, the betrayal of Gloucester and his blinding – the only alleviation to the horror being the killing of Cornwall by his servant.

Act III

As we have seen (p. 7), Charles Lamb in a famous essay contrasted the performance of *King Lear*, in which there was 'an old man tottering about the stage with a walking-stick', with the sublime impression we get from reading the storm-scenes in the privacy of the study. But this contrast loses much of its force when we realize that Lamb had never seen Shakespeare's play performed, for Tate's adaptation, with Lear's restoration and the marriage of Edgar and Cordelia, held the stage during Lamb's lifetime.

It should be noted, moreover, that stage-effects at the beginning of the nineteenth century were inevitably crude, a spurious naturalism having replaced the symbolic methods of the Elizabethans. With the introduction of electric light, the banishment of painted scenery and the use of recorded sound-effects, the storm-scenes could be presented in a more effective way than at any time since Shakespeare's death. They could be; but it must be admitted that in some modern productions the effects have got out of hand and diverted attention from the words, or even drowned them in the noise of the wind, the rain and the thunder. There was one disastrous production at Stratford-upon-Avon between the wars, in which storm-clouds projected on the cyclorama caused hilarity when the same cloud kept reappearing. A more recent production showed us Lear and the Fool seated on a pedestal which rose out of the ground and sank back after a few minutes. A commoner fault is to have the thunder so loud and so continuous that the actor playing Lear cannot be heard.

In the course of the act, Shakespeare uses the stage-direction *Storm still* six times, and this was the cue for thunder. The position of these stage-

directions makes it plain that not one of Lear's speeches is rendered
inaudible by the noise of the storm. No actor should be asked to shout
above the rain and thunder. Even if the director feels that he must insert
more thunderclaps, he can do so without doing serious damage if he
inserts them, almost as punctuation, at suitable pauses – for example, at
III.1.49 before 'Fie on this storm!'; at III.2.9 after 'ingrateful man!'
(where a thunderclap fills out a short line); and at the end of Lear's next
speech (III.2.24).

In any case, as Harley Granville-Barker, a director of genius, brilliantly
demonstrated in a preface to the play, the reality of the storm is conveyed
to the audience not by stage-effects but by the words: attempts at realism
are usually counter-productive. Therein lies the element of truth in Lamb's
diatribe. Lear acts the storm. Shakespeare, as Granville-Barker insists,
gives us 'no mere description of the storm, but in music and imaginative
suggestion a dramatic creating of the storm itself'. The madness of the
elements is reflected not merely in the madness of Lear but also in the
professional madness of the Fool, the feigned possession of Poor Tom,
and the near-madness of Gloucester, who is half crazed with grief at what
he thinks is the treachery of his beloved son.

One other preliminary point should be mentioned. There is a masterly
alternation of scenes outside (1, 2, 4 and 6) with those inside Gloucester's
castle.

Scene 1

The two functions of this scene are to prepare us for the appearance of
Lear in the storm and to inform us of Cordelia's plans. She had told Kent
in her letter that she was 'seeking to give losses their remedies'. The
Gentleman is presumably one of Lear's knights, the rest having temporarily disappeared from the play in order to emphasize the isolation of the
king: we next hear of them at III.7.15. The Gentleman's speech describes
both the king and the storm. In his 'little world of man' (the microcosm)
there is a storm which reflects, or is reflected by, the storm in the universe
(the macrocosm). The fury of Lear, urging on the storm, is duplicated by
the 'eyeless rage', the blind fury, of the winds. Man becomes part of the
elements, and the elements are given human attributes. The speech thus
prepares us for the personification of the storm and for its embodiment
in Lear.

Kent reveals that he is disguised – 'I am a gentleman of blood and
breeding' – and backs up this confession with a purse and a ring. He
discloses to the Gentleman that there is a threat of war between Albany

and Cornwall, and mentions the activities of French spies and the landing of an invading army. He asks the Gentleman to hasten to Dover and to get in touch with Cordelia. There is no need to speculate on the sources of Kent's information. Shakespeare is deliberately telescoping events; but we could surmise that the information had been contained in those parts of Cordelia's letter which were not read out when Kent was in the stocks. Since Gloucester, too, had received a letter, we get the impression that there is a regular flow of communication between France and those loyal to Lear; but Shakespeare is being obscure by design, rather than through carelessness.

It should be noted that Kent's account differs in the two basic texts of the play (see p. 68). In the Quarto there is mention of the French landing, but not of the spies. In the Folio, on the other hand, the spies are mentioned, but not the invasion. Gary Taylor has argued[4] that the second version was intended as a substitute for the first, and that we ought not to conflate them. It was important not to give the impression that the French king had invaded Britain before he could have heard of the treatment of his father-in-law. Audiences would nevertheless assume that the cruelty of Gonerill and Regan had provoked the invasion. Shakespeare often plays tricks with time.

If we followed the Folio text and omitted lines 30 to 42 with their crucial reference to Dover, the lines about Cordelia (46–9) would be puzzling, since the audience would not know that she was in Britain. On the whole, therefore, it is probably best to retain the Quarto lines. The motive of nearly all the Folio cuts seems to have been merely to shorten the play; but here Shakespeare may have feared the audience's patriotic reaction to the idea of a French invasion.

Scene 2

Lear, as we have seen, personifies the storm. He imagines it with puffed-out cheeks, like pictures of the winds at the corners of old maps, with rumbling belly, and with a mouth to spit; and the more he turns the storm into a person, the more he himself is identified with the storm.

In this scene, as in Act II, Lear's attitudes shift continually and bewilderingly. At first he wants not merely to destroy mankind, but to punish its ingratitude by destroying the possibility of rebirth by germination (8–9). So Macbeth, confronting the weird sisters, conjures them to answer his questions, 'though the treasure/ Of Nature's germens tumble all together/Even till destruction sicken.' Immediately afterwards Lear tells the elements, the instruments of the gods, that he does not accuse them of unkindness (lack of feeling for their kind) or of ingratitude to himself; but he calls them 'servile ministers' (slavish tools) for joining with his daughters to attack him. His next change of mood confirms a determination to be patient and silent (37) – some of the audience would remember that Jesus was said to be the pattern of patience, and that he answered not his accusers. Lear next addresses the gods and asks them to use the storm to terrify secret sinners into confessing their wickedness. He has moved away from his obsession with the ingratitude of his daughters to the question of all kinds of sin. The dreadful summoners call them to judgement in a kind of preview of Doomsday.

Lear himself for the first time admits that he too is a sinner, but 'More sinned against than sinning'. Soon afterwards, as many critics have suggested, he takes another step in the process of regeneration; he takes note of the sufferings of the Fool: 'I have one part in my heart/That's sorry yet for thee.' The hovel, whose shelter Kent urges the king to take, makes him reflect that 'The art of our necessities is strange/And can make vile things precious.'

He is becoming aware of the common humanity he shares with the menial, the poor and the outcast, and is prepared for his encounter with Poor Tom. The Fool's comment on the art of our necessities is to adapt the final song from *Twelfth Night*: the man with a tiny wit (such as Lear) must be contented with the resulting ill-fortune. The wind and the rain, which provide a faint undertone of melancholy at the end of *Twelfth Night*, here take on a more immediate significance. By reminding the audience of his role as Feste, Armin may more easily step out of the frame of the play to make his prophecy directly to them. (The passage is not in the Quarto, and this has made some editors argue that it is an interpolation. It is not beyond the literary powers of Armin, but it may well be Shakespeare's. Hunter, following previous editors, has rearranged the lines so that those describing the state of affairs in Lear's time, and in Shakespeare's, are separated from those which describe an ideal future, a time that was in the future for Merlin, for Lear, for Shakespeare – and for us.)

The lines on which this prophecy is partly based were printed in Thynne's edition of Chaucer and in Puttenham's *Arte of English Poesie* (1589). As Puttenham uses the word 'realm', whereas Thynne has 'londe', it seems probable that Shakespeare was following the former. But it should be noted that the original lines contain only satirical comments on an evil state of affairs – priests' lack of faith, lords' tyranny, lechery. It is the Fool who looks forward to an ideal commonwealth. Merlin is supposed to have lived more than a thousand years after Lear, and a thousand years before Shakespeare. The prophecy of a better time was still unfulfilled after two thousand years. The purpose of the deliberate anachronism, we can hardly doubt, was to remind the audience that although Lear lived before the birth of Christ, the world described in the play was relevant to those who lived in the first half of the seventeenth century, with its decline of faith, its commercial corruption, its sexual licence and its injustice. One wonders whether Shakespeare approved of the burning of heretics – the last one was put to death for heresy two years after Shakespeare's death – or merely thought the practice was preferable to the spread of the pox.

Scenes 3 and 5

These two brief scenes may conveniently be discussed together. They are in prose, except for Edmund's soliloquy at the end of III.3. They reveal once more the strength of his ambition and his apparent freedom from any scruples. His hypocrisy, which he obviously enjoys exercising, is displayed here in his pretence of being shocked by the way Lear has been treated (III.3.6) and in his pretence of disinterested loyalty when he betrays his father to Cornwall (III.5.20–22). Equally odious is Cornwall's promise of fatherly affection in the same scene, since it follows the sinister remark, 'True or false, it hath made thee Earl of Gloucester.'

Edmund's father finally decides to support the king, partly because he is genuinely shocked at the 'unnatural dealing' (words borrowed from the source), partly because the French army has landed (a circumstance which puts pressure on him to take sides), but ultimately because he knows it is right: 'If I die for it, as no less is threatened me, the King my old master must be relieved' (III.3.17–18). Obviously his motives are mixed (as all motives tend to be) but in this decision he finally abandons the position of neutrality. Because of his gullibility and of Edmund's treachery, his decision has fatal consequences. Even relieving the king involved disobedience to his overlord, Cornwall; and to be in communication with the invader was treasonable. But treason is sometimes the right course.

Scene 4

It is in this scene that Lear crosses the frontier of madness. We can trace the steps by which this comes about. Before the end of Act II he had had a premonition that he would go mad. In Act III he welcomes the storm, terrifying as it is, because it takes his mind off the obsession, which is driving him mad, of filial ingratitude. Then he concerns himself with the greater physical sufferings of the Fool, and this leads him to a prayer ('I'll pray and then I'll sleep'). But he prays not to the gods this time, but to the poor naked wretches for whose sufferings he had given too little thought when he had the power to relieve them. It is significant that the idea of sharing superfluity with the poor to achieve a fairer society is echoed by Gloucester (IV.1) when he gives his purse to Poor Tom. He too wants distribution to undo excess, so that everyone may have enough. The repetition should be enough to disprove the view that Lear's awakened social conscience is a sign of insanity. A fair society, which would show the heavens more just, can be brought about only by the actions of men, and Lear prays to and for the impoverished members of society. The physic which pomp is bidden to take to cure it of its superflux, the disease from which it is suffering, is a fairer distribution of wealth. This cures both the poor (who have too little) and the rich (who have too much). This is the exact opposite of a tax policy which is designed to make the rich richer and the poor poorer.

When the Fool enters the hovel he is terrified by the apparition of Poor Tom, whose first cry ('Fathom and half, fathom and half!') is suggested by the waterlogged state of the hovel. Kent takes the Fool's hand to comfort him – a nice touch. It is the sight of the nearly naked Tom that drives Lear mad. Meeting the feigned madman enables him to escape into insanity; but the world of his madness is nevertheless filled with thoughts he is trying to escape. He at once assumes that the reason why Poor Tom is destitute must be that he, like Lear, has given all to his daughters.

On one level Edgar puts on a superb performance as a Bedlam beggar. He complicates the role by making him a demoniac and giving him a plausible case-history. There are more than a score of echoes from Harsnet's exposure of the counterfeit demoniacs in this one scene, and many more in III.6 (see p. 83). That they were counterfeit, and attacked by Harsnet for their play-acting, makes Edgar's task easier – he is counterfeiting a counterfeit. He mingles snatches of nonsense, bawdy, scraps of proverbial wisdom, echoes from the Bible, lines from forgotten poems, bits of doggerel, all mixed up together. His most coherent speech is like a confession at a revivalist meeting: he describes his career as a servingman and gives a lurid inventory of his vices; he was lustful, proud, vain, murderous, greedy, treacherous and prodigal. Some of these characteristics may remind us of Oswald, a servingman who served the lust of his mistress's heart, if only by acting as a go-between.

Confronted with Poor Tom's nakedness, Lear meditates on man's essential being. Stripped of his clothes, he is merely 'a poor, bare, forked animal'. This speech links up with the earlier one on clothes (II.4.259), and the later one on the way in which robes and furred gowns conceal vices (IV.6.166). As we have seen (p. 17), there are several passages in Florio's translation of Montaigne's essays which contrast the defencelessness of man with the protection of animals by wool, hide and feathers – '... man only (oh silly wretched man) can neither go [i.e. walk] nor speak, nor shift, nor feed himself, unless it be to whine and weep only, except he be taught'. Montaigne provides a list of borrowings from the other animals, the idea that our clothes are 'lendings', and the word 'sophisticated'.

Presumably the Fool does not intend his reference to an old lecher's heart to apply to Gloucester, though the audience will make the connection. Gloucester does not recognize Edgar, but Edgar overhears his father's confession of grief and love. The tribute to Kent's prophetic insight is spoken unknowingly to Kent himself; and Gloucester's confession that grief has crazed his wits makes him join the other three representatives of madness. As the Fool had prophesied, 'This cold night will turn us all to fools and madmen.' The madness of the storm and the four sorts of human madness 'together exemplify the break-up of society and the threat to the universe itself under the impact of filial ingratitude and treachery'.[5]

Lear in his madness takes Poor Tom for a philosopher, on the assumption that only the most dejected creature, one who has nothing superfluous, can instruct him on the essential nature of man. Instead of accepting that the gods are responsible for thunder, Lear asks one of the favourite questions in philosophical dialogues: 'What is the cause of thunder?' and then enquires about Poor Tom's field of research. At the end of the scene he refuses to be separated from his 'learnèd Theban', his 'good Athenian'. It was shown by Edmund Blunden in an ingenious essay[6] that the link in Shakespeare's mind between the two was a passage in one of Horace's *Epistles* (II.1) on the power of a great poet to transport us instantaneously in imagination from Athens to Thebes (*'et modo me Thebis, modo ponit Athenis'*) and that the repetition of *modo* in this line, and hence the whole passage, was triggered off by the name of one of the devils – Modo – mentioned ten lines earlier. Another link was provided by Harsnet, who quoted and translated a passage from Horace's next epistle; and passages in both epistles mention terrors and magic.

Scene 6

A large part of this scene, including the whole of the mock trial of Gonerill and Regan, was omitted from the Folio text. This cut has been thought to indicate that the scene did not go down well with the audience, but it is more probable that, like the other cuts (see p. 115–16), it was made for the sole purpose of reducing the length of the play. Of course the presentation of madness in the theatre was made more difficult in Shakespeare's day by the fact that people visited Bedlam to be entertained by the antics of the lunatics. When Dekker depicted a mad scene in *The Honest Whore* (Part 1), he was careful to prepare for it, so that the audience would receive it seriously:

> And though 'twould grieve a soul, to see God's image
> So blemish'd and defac'd, yet do they act
> Such antic and such pretty lunacies
> That spite of sorrow they will make you smile.

Dekker, for all his humane and sensible instincts, was apt to sentimentalize reality. Shakespeare does not pretend that the lunacies he depicts are pretty; but he gives us opportunities to laugh at the jests of the Fool and the gibberish of Poor Tom. This diverts our laughter from Lear himself. The responses of the audience are directed by Kent's solicitude: 'Will you lie down and rest upon the cushings?', and 'O pity! Sir, where is the patience now/That you so oft have boasted to retain?' They are directed, too, by Edgar's one aside: 'My tears begin to take his part so much/They mar my counterfeiting.'

The scene immediately follows Cornwall's resolve to punish Gloucester, so that Kent's words, 'The gods reward your kindness!', must strike the audience with bitter irony, although they do not know precisely what his 'reward' is going to be.

Hunter replied in advance to recent critics who rejoiced in the deletion of this scene. He declared that

The antiphonally placed voices of the three madmen – lunatic King, court fool, feigned Bedlam – weave the obsessive themes of betrayal, demoniac possession, and injustice into the most complex lyric structure in modern drama.

The Fool's examples of madness are really only of foolishness, or lack of worldly wisdom: 'He's mad that trusts in the tameness of a wolf, a horse's health, a boy's love, or a whore's oath.'

Meanwhile Poor Tom is concerned with devils (Fraterretto, Hoppedance, the foul fiend) and the hell from which they come. Nero, one of the wickedest of Roman emperors, an incestuous matricide, would have been suggested by the fiddler in hell mentioned by Harsnet – everyone knows that he fiddled while Rome burned. His angling comes from Chaucer: 'Nettes of gold threed hadde he greet plentee/To fisshe in Tybre, when hym liste pleye', and the lake of darkness conflates Harsnet's 'Stygian lake' and references to the bottomless pit with the knowledge that Nero attempted to sound the depth of the Alcyonian Lake, through which Dionysus went to hell to fetch up Semele. Reminded of the tortures of hell, Lear proposes to have a thousand devils 'with red burning spits/Come hissing in upon' his daughters. Then punishment leads to the idea of judgement, and he decides to bring Gonerill and Regan to trial before a bench of judges. Poor Tom's blanket and the Fool's motley appear to him as judicial robes, so he addresses them as 'most learnèd' and 'sapient'. The symbolic significance of the trial of the mighty and powerful by the outcast and simple is sufficiently obvious. Lear, as prosecutor and witness, accuses Gonerill not of her actual offences but of a symbolic crime: 'she kicked the poor King her father'. In this substitution, with uncanny prescience Shakespeare hit on one characteristic of mental derangement held crucial by modern medical science. Regan's warped looks are a reminder of the contrast between Lear's illusions about her (II.4.65ff.) – that her nature is 'tender-hefted' and her eyes comforting – and the reality of her actual character.

When Lear ceases to imagine that he sees Gonerill and Regan they vanish, and he accuses the judges of letting them escape. But when he returns to the subject of Regan he wants to know if there is 'any cause in nature that makes these hard hearts' (75–7). This remark is prompted by Poor Tom's 'thy horn is dry' – as though he supposed that Regan's heart had become as hard as horn. Is she wicked, or merely diseased?

Poor Tom's blanket now appears, absurdly, to be a Persian robe. Shakespeare remembers Horace's best-known ode (I.35) in which he objects to Persian attire; and this memory blends with an equally familiar biblical phrase 'that it be not changed, according to the law of the Medes and Persians which altereth not'.

The last words of the Fool – 'And I'll go to bed at noon' – are primarily a reply to Lear's 'We'll go to supper i' the morning'; another example of the topsy-turvy state of affairs. But Edmund Blunden extracted several other meanings from the words, including a suggestion of premature death. The Fool fades out of the play when he helps to carry Lear out to the waiting litter. It is useless to speculate on his fate. That he dies of pneumonia or tuberculosis is the favourite assumption of directors; that he is caught and hanged is the theory of those who misinterpret Lear's last speech. That Lear, being mad, can now act as his own fool is another suggestion; and that the actor has to change his costume in order to play the part of Cordelia is a fourth. In Kozintsev's film he survives to the end. Now that Lear is mad, the Fool's functions – to cheer him, to criticize him, to keep him sane – no longer operate. He therefore disappears.

Gloucester enters (84) with the news that there is a plot to murder

Lear. The daughters and Cornwall have gone beyond the cold-hearted ingratitude of the previous act. The king is hurried out and Edgar is left to soliloquize in rhymed couplets on the situation. These lines are not in the Folio text, and those who believe that Shakespeare himself was responsible for the cut congratulate him on his wisdom in omitting such explicit moral commentary. But we should remember that during the whole of Act III Edgar has been speaking as Poor Tom (except for a line and a half spoken aside). The soliloquy is therefore important for the actor as a means of re-establishing Edgar's identity. He plays so many parts in the course of the play that we are liable to lose sight of the man behind the various masks he wears. He has had no opportunity of telling us what he now feels about his father. The lines, moreover, contain two vital dramatic points. They make the first verbal link between plot and sub-plot in the words 'He childed as I fathered', and they emphasize that the mental suffering of the king is harder to bear than the physical suffering of the beggar. Edgar, too, has had more than his share of mental suffering in being rejected by the father he loves. That he is able to say: 'How light and portable my pain seems now' exhibits his remarkable capacity to feel the griefs of others. As he puts it later (IV.6.222–3), 'by the art of known and feeling sorrows' he is 'pregnant to good pity'. (Some critics regard Edgar with refined distaste, as saints are often regarded by the unregenerate.)

The speech is in rhyme to indicate that it should not be taken naturalistically but rather as a choric comment on the action by one who is a frequent commentator, leading the responses of the audience, besides being one who plays a leading part in the action.

Scene 7

In *Arcadia*, Sidney does not describe the blinding of the Paphlagonian king: he mentions the deed in only four words. Possibly Shakespeare remembered the scene in *Selimus*, as Inga-Stina Ewbank suggested. This was a play printed in 1594 and ascribed by Grosart to Robert Greene. In it Acomat pulls out Aga's eyes on stage. But after his first tragedy, *Titus Andronicus*, Shakespeare generally avoided horrific scenes. The princes in *Richard III* are murdered off stage, and so is Duncan; Julius Caesar and Desdemona have to die on stage, as everyone would agree. But it is worth asking why Shakespeare decided to stage the blinding of Gloucester. In the first place, he may well have thought that a description of the blinding would not have the same impact on his audience as its presentation on stage, and that a sensational and horrific effect was necessary if the incident were not to seem an anti-climax after the storm-scenes. Then, as we have seen (p. 36), the spiritual blindness of Gloucester, his inability to see clearly in the early acts of the play, which he himself acknowledges in the words 'I stumbled when I saw', is one of the two paradoxes on which the play is constructed; and Edgar later connects his father's adultery with his blinding: 'The dark and vicious place where thee he got/Cost him his eyes.'

The imagery connected with sight, from the first scene to the last, moves out of metaphor into fact in the blinding scene. Shakespeare, as Stewart pointed out, achieved 'the powerful effect of a suddenly realized imagery: the oppressive atmosphere of the play here condensing into a ghastly dew'. The extreme horror was a necessary part of Shakespeare's purpose: he wanted us to be fully conscious of the wickedness of the perpetrators. Replying to criticisms that the poet made concessions to the demand for sensationalism, Raleigh remarked[7] that they were 'transmuted in the giving, so that what might have been a mere connivance in baseness becomes a miracle of expressive art'.

In spite of the threatened hostility between Cornwall and Albany and the sex-rivalry which is developing between Gonerill and Regan, they are temporarily united in face of the French invasion, and they exchange hollow endearments – 'dear sister', 'sweet lord'. We are soon shown that Gloucester has been condemned without trial. Here, as in Scene 5, Cornwall talks of revenge rather than of justice, and he admits that what he is about to do is illegal. It is also a terrible violation of hospitality, as Gloucester points out. Regan, whom Lear thought of as tender, emerges as cruel and sadistic. She throws at Gloucester the epithet we know to be appropriate to herself – 'ingrateful'. She tears white hairs from his beard, is clearly excited by the blinding, demanding the gouging out of the other eye, and she relishes administering the shock to Gloucester that he had been betrayed by Edmund.

The interrogation, with its thrice-repeated 'Wherefore to Dover?' and Regan's 'let him smell/His way to Dover', are enough to explain why the victim decides to make his way there. It is true that the congregation at Dover of all the surviving characters of both plots was a dramatic necessity; but as Bradley complained, Gloucester did not need to go to Dover to commit suicide. Yet Shakespeare provides a psychological reason for Gloucester's choice of Dover. Apart from the fact that the king's friends would be drawn to Dover where Cordelia was known to be, the traumatic experience of the blinding comes immediately after the reiterated shouts of the interrogators, and Dover was firmly fixed in Gloucester's mind as a place of refuge or rest.

Realizing that he is doomed, and expecting to be killed, Gloucester bursts out with a denunciation of his captors for their treatment of the anointed king:

> Because I would not see thy cruel nails
> Pluck out his poor old eyes; nor thy fierce sister
> In his anointed flesh rash boarish fangs.
> The sea, with such a storm as his bare head
> In hell-black night endured, would have buoyed up
> And quenched the stellèd fires;
> Yet, poor old heart, he holp the heavens to rain.
> If wolves had at thy gate howled that dern time
> Thou shouldst have said, 'Good porter, turn the key;
> All cruels else subscribe'. But I shall see
> The wingèd Vengeance overtake such children.

There is irony in his fear that Regan would pluck out Lear's eyes as he does not suspect the fate in store for himself, and more irony in the last sentence. The speech is significant for its comparisons with wild beasts. Gonerill is compared with a wild boar and both sisters are said to be more cruel to their father than they would be to wolves. As we have seen (p. 38), sixty-four different animals are mentioned in the course of the play. Sometimes, as in III.4, human beings in their weakness are contrasted with animals in their strength; but more often, as here, it is the evil characters who are compared with wild beasts.

The first person to propose the blinding is Gonerill, though the idea is taken up enthusiastically by Cornwall and Regan, simply because the punishment is crueller than a simple execution. It turns out to be a disastrous mistake, as Regan later admits, because the atrocity makes the perpetrators unpopular. More immediately it leads to the revolt of one of Cornwall's own servants, and to Cornwall's fatal wound. This in turn leads to the fatal rivalry between the two sisters for Edmund, and ultimately to the miserable death of all the evil characters. The humanity and courage of Cornwall's servant have far-reaching consequences.

The dialogue at the end of the scene between the surviving servants – the dead one is to be thrown on a dunghill – is omitted from the Folio text. It has been argued unconvincingly that Shakespeare was responsible for the cut, that the moralizing is unnecessary since all decent people will deplore the conduct of the villains, and that the plan to get Poor Tom to act as a guide seems to be contradicted by what happens in the next scene, where Gloucester himself asks Poor Tom to lead him. (They might have added that, as Edgar would have kept away from the castle, the servants would not have known of the existence of this Poor Tom.)

Shakespeare's plays are full of similar discrepancies, which are not noticed in performance. Indeed, slight changes of plan actually increase the sense that the events are real and not ingenious artefacts. Audiences, moreover, are not bored by being told how horribly the villains have behaved: they need to have their feelings of outrage expressed by characters in the play. As Philip Edwards has pointed out:

> The moment of stillness provided by the shock and compassion of the servants ... is a theatrical experience of the highest order. Whoever cut the scene failed to grasp its theatrical imaginativeness as well as its thematic importance, and he could hardly have been Shakespeare.

There is another powerful and practical reason why the dialogue should not be cut, as I realized during the two productions with which I have been associated. Gloucester leaves the stage at line 93. If the servants' dialogue is cut, he has to re-enter only nine lines later in a different costume, and possibly with bandaged eyes. This is not long enough. Even if there were a substantial interval between the acts, which would make a long play nearly twice the standard length, I think the cut would be disastrous. If Shakespeare made it, or even agreed to it, the less Shakespeare he.

It is significant that Peter Brook, in his stage production as well as in his film, omitted the lines; for, under the influence of Jan Kott, who regarded the play as Shakespeare's *End Game*, or because he wished to show Shakespeare's affinities with the Theatre of Cruelty, he deliberately cut those lines which expressed humanity or compassion. It is not always realized that even in the grimmest of Shakespearian tragedies the good characters outnumber the bad.

Act IV

Lear is absent from the stage from III.6 to IV.6.80. This is in accordance with Shakespeare's normal, but not invariable, practice. Hamlet is off the stage, supposedly on board ship, for most of Act IV, while Ophelia goes mad, Claudius and Laertes hatch their plot against him, and Fortinbras conquers Poland. During the fourth act of *Macbeth* Lady Macduff and her children are murdered and, in the long scene at the English court, Macduff and Malcolm unite against Macbeth, who does not reappear until the second scene of Act V. The practice does not merely give a much-needed rest to the leading actors, but enables the counter-action to be developed. In *King Lear*, Edgar repays his father's ill-treatment of him, as Cordelia repays hers, with filial care. He acts as his guide and averts his suicide. Cordelia arrives in Britain to succour the father who has banished her. The strife between Albany and Cornwall is succeeded by the struggle between Gonerill and Regan for Edmund's favours.

Scene 1

Edgar in his last soliloquy (III.6) had found his suffering bearable because the king's was worse. In his first speech in the present scene, he seems almost happy. He assumes that as he has experienced the worst that can befall him, any change must be for the better. He soon realizes his error. He is confronted with the sight of his father and is forced to confess that he has been too sanguine: 'I am worse than e'er I was.'

There is a controversy about the text of line 10, and this may serve as a single example of the many problems connected with the text of the play – whether we should follow Quarto or Folio (see p. 115), and what to do when neither seems to make satisfactory sense. Quarto in its uncorrected state read *poorlie, leed*; and Folio, derived from this, corrected it to *poorly led*, meaning, presumably, 'led by a poor man'. But Quarto in its corrected state, which the Folio editor did not see, read *parti, eyd*; and this is the basis for Hunter's reading *parti-eyed*, which he explains as 'having his eyes looking like a fool's coat in the red of blood and the white of eggs' (applied by Cornwall's servants, as they had promised). This seems somewhat forced, and one doubts if an audience would understand it. Now Sidney describes the blind king as *poorly arrayed*, and it is possible that Shakespeare wrote this and then deleted the initial letter of *arayd* with a vertical stroke, which, as Janet Leeper surmised, could have been mistaken for the 'l' of *leed*, as *rayd* could have been misread as *eyd*. It is easy to understand that a proofreader, aware of the blinding, would be influenced by this in his attempt to decipher the manuscript. This is not the only suggested emendation for this line, but it will illustrate the problems.

Gloucester's confession, 'I stumbled when I saw', with the corollary that he is wiser now that he has been blinded, is, as we have seen, one of the central paradoxes of the play (see p. 36), and it is followed by the generalization that 'our mere defects/Prove our commodities'. He is, in fact, wiser not because he has lost his eyes but because he has been told that Edmund had betrayed him, and that therefore Edgar had been maligned and cast out on the word of a villain.

Gloucester's new wisdom is made apparent by his concern for the safety of the Old Man, who may suffer from association with a traitor, and in his new humility ('Do as I bid thee, or rather do thy pleasure'). Edgar

89

learns that his father now knows of his innocence when he hears the words:

> O dear son Edgar,
> The food of thy abusèd father's wrath!
> Might I but live to see thee in my touch
> I'd say I had eyes again.

And presumably Edgar deduces that he, like his father, had been betrayed by Edmund. Gloucester mentions that he had thought of Edgar when he saw Poor Tom in the storm; 'and yet my mind/Was then scarce friends with him.' This introduces his notorious complaint about the cruelty of the gods:

> I have heard more since.
> As flies to wanton boys, are we to the gods;
> They kill us for their sport.

The idea is a common one. Parallels have been found in Plautus, Aeschylus, Aristophanes, Calvin, Montaigne, Sidney and many others. The lines are often taken to be the keynote of the play, and even to express Shakespeare's personal view not merely of this play but of life in general. It is, however, important to remember that Gloucester's blinding and Cordelia's murder are carried out by men, and that the words are spoken immediately after the blinding, when Gloucester is suffering not merely great physical pain but the worse mental agony of learning that he has cast out his beloved son on the evidence of a villain. Moreover, later in this act Gloucester addresses the gods not as sadistic monsters, but as 'ever-gentle' (IV.6.217). We can take neither remark as his considered opinion. Nor should one assume that remarks made by any of Shakespeare's characters express his personal views, still less when the spokesman has been a credulous, superstitious adulterer. The poet is more likely to choose as his spokesman characters who are portrayed sympathetically, and who are therefore admired by the audience (see p. 44). When Thomas Hardy concluded *Tess of the D'Urbervilles* by declaring that with her execution 'the President of the Immortals finished his sport with Tess', he was expressing a view which surfaces in *The Dynasts* and in many of his novels and poems. It is therefore proper to assume that this was Hardy's own view of life – not that he believed in the existence of gods or God, but rather that human beings are frustrated by the nature of things, and that they struggle in vain with a blind fate. A novelist in commenting on the action carries out the function of a chorus, telling the reader or the audience what to think. Some dramatists do the same thing; but perhaps the greatest dramatists hide behind the masks of their characters.

Edgar willingly agrees to act as his father's guide, and it soon becomes apparent that he hopes to prevent him from committing suicide. Why he continues to conceal his identity is not explained, as it would have to be in a more naturalistic play. Edgar later admits that it was a 'fault' on his part, but in his account of Gloucester's death there is no time for him to elaborate on this point, when the audience is mainly anxious about the fate of Lear and Cordelia. The more Edgar talks, and the longer Edmund remains silent, the chance of the captives surviving is progressively diminished.

It would be possible to offer several explanations of Edgar's reluctance to reveal himself, although in performance these are irrelevant. (There is a similar reluctance by Kent.) Edgar may have thought, for example, that to guide his father without revealing his identity was the best way of reconciling him to life. He may have thought that to reveal that the son his father had cast out had been compelled to disguise himself as a Bedlam beggar would have increased Gloucester's shame at his own foolish credulity. He may have wished to prove his own manhood and avenge both himself and his father by defeating Edmund – and several other explanations have been offered. But perhaps the most important reasons for Edgar's concealment of his identity were dramatic and thematic. On the one hand Shakespeare could extract some powerful ironies from Gloucester's ignorance, as when Edgar uses the ambiguous title of 'father'. He was able to keep the audience in suspense, wondering when Edgar would confess. On the other hand, the thematic importance of the madman leading the blind, of the poor and outcast exemplifying compassion and teaching the lesson of patience and endurance, is clearly of great significance.

Edgar makes one last speech as a demoniac in this scene (55–62). Afterwards he gradually comes to speak more sanely, and in a more normal voice. Gloucester assumes that Poor Tom's destitution is caused by heaven's plagues; and, like Lear in the storm, he prays that the man with superfluous wealth should share it with the poor.

Scene 2

This scene takes place after the news of Gloucester's arrest has reached Albany, but before the news of his blinding or of the death of Cornwall. Albany, as Oswald reports, has immediately realized the evil of Gonerill and Regan in their treatment of their father, but he does not know of their plot to kill him, or of Gonerill's plot with Edmund. This is the significance of the words 'Our wishes on the way/May prove effects' (i.e. the hopes we expressed on our journey hither may be realized), and 'If you dare venture in your own behalf'. Gonerill hopes that Edmund will carry out the murder of Albany; Edmund, as we learn later, hopes that Gonerill will do it.

Too often critics (and directors) have assumed that Gonerill's indictment of Albany for his 'cowish terror' has some justification; and her patriotic speech (50–59) is regarded as a proper condemnation of Albany's spinelessness. But patriotism, as Dr Johnson reminds us, is (sometimes) the last refuge of a scoundrel, as it is with the wicked queen in *Cymbeline*. It is made perfectly plain that Albany's reluctance to fight is not due to physical cowardice but to the doubts he entertains about the right course of action. On the one hand he believes that he should repel the French invader; on the other hand, he knows that Cordelia's intervention is disinterested, and directly caused by her sisters' treatment of their father. As Albany remarks later, 'Where I could not be honest,/I never yet was valiant.' In *Troilus and Cressida* Hector is faced with a similar problem. Although he knows that Helen ought to be restored to her husband and argues to that effect, he nevertheless fights on behalf of Troy against the Greeks.

This scene is dreadfully mangled in the Folio by the omission of twenty lines, consisting of two of Albany's most eloquent denunciations of his wife. In one he speaks of her unnaturalness: 'She that herself will sliver and disbranch/From her material sap perforce must wither.' In the other he speaks of the overturning of moral order through the commission of wickedness, and of the fear, expressed by Ulysses in *Troilus and Cressida*, and in several other places in Shakespeare's plays, that the result will be chaos and even cannibalism:

> If that the heavens do not their visible spirits
> Send quickly down to tame these vile offences,
> It will come –
> Humanity must perforce prey on itself,
> Like monsters of the deep.

Without these lines and other attacks on Gonerill ('You are not worth the dust which the rude wind/Blows in your face'; 'Wisdom and goodness to the vile seem vile;/Filths savour but themselves'), Albany seems to be worsted in the slanging match. Some recent critics have brought themselves to believe that Shakespeare deliberately weakened Albany's part, although it is difficult to discover any sensible reason for so doing, unless the actor playing the part was incompetent. The cut has the effect of reducing Albany's part, but the motive, as we can see from other cuts, was simply to reduce the playing-time of the play.

After Gonerill's attack on Albany's cowardice, there is another savage cut in which he tells her not to 'be-monster' her 'feature', confesses that he would like to tear her to pieces, and that, although she is a fiend, she is saved by the fact that she has a woman's shape. Albany and Gonerill have no common ground. To Gonerill, Albany is a cowardly, moralizing fool, one who obeys the religious injunction to turn the other cheek. To Albany, Gonerill is unnatural, parricidal, tigerish and devilish. The reactions of the two to the news of Gloucester's blinding and of Cornwall's death are characteristically different. Gonerill, who had suggested the blinding, makes no comment on it; she is glad of Cornwall's death as it opens the way for her to rule a reunited kingdom; but she is afraid that Regan, now a widow, will have more chance of displacing her in Edmund's affections: she trusts neither. Albany is horrified by the blinding – he has just referred to Cornwall as his 'good' brother; he asks if Edmund was privy to it, and vows to avenge Gloucester's eyes. The killing of Cornwall seems to him a proof of divine vengeance:

> This shows you are above,
> You justicers, that these are nether crimes
> So speedily can venge!

Although the immediate cause of Cornwall's death was his anonymous servant, the gods, he assumes, have used a human instrument.

Scene 3

The whole of this scene is omitted by the Folio; and although the cut has its ardent defenders it seems to others (including myself) to be deplorable. The omission has one advantage, however. The explanation for the King of France's return to his own country is vague and feeble. In such cases silence is the best policy. Shakespeare doubtless wanted to minimize patriotic reactions to the French invasion and to make it clear that Cordelia's motives were above reproach. The Gentleman's explanation, Greg argues, 'we can hardly be intended to take ... at its face value':

> The real reason ... was that Cordelia succeeded in persuading her husband to abandon his purpose of wresting a portion of the kingdom for himself and retire to his own land, thus leaving her free to use his army in defence of her father, should the occasion arise.

This interpretation may be correct, but it would be difficult to convey it to an audience.

In any case, if the whole scene is omitted, the following one (IV.4), in which Cordelia actually appears, would lose some of its effect; for she has been absent from the stage for some two thousand lines; Lear has not mentioned her since the end of the first act. Kent, it is true, has referred to her twice. But she has fewer words to speak than almost any major character in all Shakespeare's plays: her entry in the next scene needs preparation. The account of her reading the letter about the treatment of Lear by Gonerill and Regan fills out our knowledge of her and of her saintly character. To some critics the description of her tears is 'mannered'. It is in the Arcadian style which Shakespeare used again in the plays of the last period, and forms an essential counterbalance to the violence of the language and actions of the preceding scenes. The scene also throws light on Kent and his love and reverence for Cordelia. Moreover the revelation that Lear is so ashamed of his treatment of Cordelia that he refuses to meet her prepares the way for their reconciliation when it takes place in IV.7. It should be noticed that Lear has lucid intervals, when he is in his 'better tune'.

Scene 4

Just as IV.3 was designed to prepare the way for Cordelia's entrance, so this scene prepares us for Lear's entrance in IV.6, wearing a crown of weeds. He has escaped from Kent's supervision and, surprisingly, he has been heard singing. (Ophelia in her madness is also given to singing, even in her last moments.) The Doctor's prescription for the cure of Lear's insanity – of rest induced by sleep-producing drugs – is seconded by Cordelia's prayer for 'blest natural secrets', watered by her tears of love; and this prepares us for the scene in which Lear is awakened by music, from sleep into sanity.

The comparison of Cordelia's tears with holy water in the previous scene and the tears of love in this scene combine to give the impression of her natural sanctity; and it can hardly be doubted that in the lines in which she claims that the motive for the invasion is not for conquest, but to succour her father, Shakespeare intended the echo of Jesus's first recorded words (Luke 2:49):

> O dear father,
> It is thy business that I go about.

Scene 5

The mention of the approach of the British forces in Cordelia's last speech is taken up in Regan's first words. The war is suggested with remarkable economy because only the results are important. When the battle comes, it is not even described. Shakespeare is equally economical in his treatment of the rivalry between Regan and Gonerill for Edmund's love. Regan tries unsuccessfully to undermine Oswald's loyalty to her sister (see p. 25). Her hypocrisy is neatly revealed in her pretence that Edmund has gone in search of his father, in order to kill him on humanitarian grounds, 'In pity of his misery'. She has confessed to Oswald, only a moment before, that the sight of the blinded Gloucester stirs up feeling against the perpetrators, and immediately afterwards she admits that Edmund has gone on a reconnaissance expedition to assess the enemy's strength. Regan is so inveterately hypocritical that she cannot drop the habit when talking to Oswald.

Scene 6

This powerful and varied scene is more important thematically than for its advancement of the action, but there is nevertheless plenty of action. It begins with Gloucester's attempted suicide, and is followed by the encounter between the mad Lear and the blind Gloucester, Edgar's slaying of Oswald while defending his father (who still wants to die), and the discovery of Gonerill's plot to have her husband murdered.

[1–80]   Edgar, in the 'best apparel' of Gloucester's tenant, has dropped the Bedlam patter and his feigned possession by devils (but see line 79). As Gloucester realizes, he is better-spoken than he was. His description of Dover cliff is so vivid that it has imposed on critics as well as on Gloucester. They are not on the cliffs at all but, as we discover later, on, or near, the beach (see line 272).

It has recently been suggested that Shakespeare took some details of the scene from the account given by Spenser of the one-eyed miser, Malbecco, in *The Faerie Queene* (III.x.56), who

>   ... came unto a rockie hill
> Over the sea, suspended dreadfully,
> That living creature it would terrify
> To looke adowne, or upward to the height ...
> But through long anguish, and selfe-murdring thought
> He was so wasted and forpined quight,

> That all his substance was consum'd to nought,
> And nothing left, but like an aery Spright,
> That on the rockes he fell so flit and light,
> That he thereby receiv'd no hurt at all.

The mock suicide is often regarded as a prime example of the grotesque element in the play, an example of the absurd, and it is assumed that the audience would regard the episode as comic. 'Comic' in a sense it may be, yet never once in all the productions I have seen, or in those in which I have been actively involved, have I heard even a single laugh. Gloucester is protected both by the pathos of his situation and by the deep concern of Edgar lest his experiment should fail. As Susan Snyder says,

> In the stage conditions for which it was written, this scene gives not just a spectacle of absurdity, but an experience of it. Ideally we should be 'with' Gloucester as he prepares solemnly for his end, right up to the moment when the abortive leap violently separates our perspective from his.

Edgar succeeds, still without revealing his identity, in persuading Gloucester not to renew his attempt at suicide, and in altering his view that the gods are cruel to a nominal admission that they are kindly. The change is brought about by Edgar's persuasion and by his pretence that Gloucester has been preserved by a miracle: 'Think that the clearest gods, who make them honours/Of men's impossibilities, have preserved thee.' He is made to believe that he was tempted to commit suicide by a fiend, or by one who was possessed by devils. Gloucester has been deceived: the miracle is a trick. But Edgar's virtuous deceit for a good end contrasts with his brother's evil deceit for his own personal advantage, and parallels Cordelia's doctor-like attention to her father.

Before the end of the scene Gloucester prays for death and wishes he were mad, like the king, so as not to be fully conscious of his 'huge sorrows'. But he thanks his rescuer, who calls him 'father', a word which has one meaning for Gloucester and another for Edgar.

Edgar has assumed another persona, this time of a perfectly normal peasant, 'A most poor man made tame to fortune's blows'; and in his encounter with Oswald he puts on a rustic accent – an all-purpose stage rustic accent – so as not to reveal his identity. There is a price on his head as well as on Gloucester's.

[80–203]   When Lear enters, Shakespeare is careful to direct our responses in relation to Lear's grotesque madness. Edgar's three remarks, in particular his comment that the king's ravings consist of mingled sense and nonsense ('matter and impertinency'), warn us to take their content seriously and not as mere ravings, while Gloucester's reverence, and his comparison of Lear, a 'ruined piece of nature', with the approaching end of the world, have the effect of magnifying the king and his significance. On the other hand, the crown of weeds carries a suggestion of second-childishness (and possibly of a victim adorned for the sacrifice) and suggests an intimacy with a benevolent nature unperverted by human evil.

As critics have recognized, Lear's apparently disconnected remarks are linked by subconscious logic and by hidden puns. 'Touch', for example, means 'arrest' and 'test gold'; this thought leads to coining, and the idea that the king cannot be counterfeited as his image on the coin can be. Coin leads to the press-money paid to soldiers, and hence to their erratic shooting, and so on. In Lear's next speech, the white beard of Gloucester, whom he does not recognize until much later, reminds him of Gonerill's flattery of his white hair. He knows that, like all kings, he has been flattered all his life. Then his half-remembrance of Gloucester and his sons leads to his pardon of adultery but also to the denunciation of female sexuality. This is linked with Lear's earlier threat to divorce himself from the tomb of Regan's mother because it sepulchres an adulteress (II.4.126–7), and also with the mincing affectation of virtue, the assumed prudishness of Gonerill in her attacks on the riotous behaviour of Lear's knights. As the audience has observed the lecherous rivalry between the sisters for Edmund's favours, unknown to Lear, the attack on the animality of women will come with additional force. Shakespeare appears to have taken some hints from the sordid details of exorcisms, as recounted by Harsnet; and the idea of centaurs, half human, half animal, supports Heilman's remark about Gonerill and Regan: 'The paradox is that these free minds, unburdened by any conventional or traditional allegiances, become slaves to the uncontrolled animal desire.' (See reference to Ixion, p. 101).

As some critics have supposed that 'the primitive revulsion against sex' displayed in Lear's diatribe is an expression of Shakespeare's own, if temporary, feelings, it may be necessary to question such an interpretation. Although in the *Sonnets* Shakespeare wrote of his relations with the so-called Dark Lady as 'the expense of spirit in a waste of shame' and in *Timon of Athens* made his bachelor hero inveigh against female promiscuity and expatiate on the ravages of venereal disease, it should be remembered that the experience recorded in the *Sonnets* (if not purely fictional) had taken place many years previously; between it and the writing of *King Lear* many comedies had intervened. No one could pretend that the sexuality of Portia, Rosalind, Viola and Olivia was at all tainted; and if Hamlet attacks Gertrude's sexuality and his love for Ophelia is blighted by his sense of disgust, and if Othello blames the 'cause' which drives him to murder the innocent Desdemona, these are a direct result of the situations in which the heroes find themselves. Hamlet may generalize that 'frailty's name is woman'; Shakespeare does not. So Lear's attitudes are partly determined by the situation and partly by the common knowledge that some forms of madness were expressed in this way. This is obvious in Ophelia's case, for though her madness was brought on by Hamlet's treatment of her as well as by her father's death, her obscenities are clearly out of character.

Elizabethan dramatists usually used prose for the speech of mad persons (for example, Titus, Ophelia, and Hieronimo in *The Spanish Tragedy*). Lear moves in and out of prose, using a form of verse in his more coherent moments. But it is verse of great irregularity, so irregular that the Quarto compositor not unnaturally assumed that all Lear's speeches in this scene were in prose. There are eight short lines between lines 110 and 127, and editors invariably disagree about the arrangement of the lines, and whether passages should be printed as verse or prose. It does not greatly matter; but as far as I know it has not been pointed out that in the same passage the lines are linked together by concealed rhymes (here in italics):

> *Die* for adultery? *No.*
> The wren *goes* to't, and the small gilded *fly*
> Does lecher in my *sight*.
> Let copula*tion* thrive; for Gloucester's bastard *son*
> Was kinder to his father than my daughters
> Got 'tween the lawful sheets.
> To't, luxury, pell-mell, for I lack *sold*iers.
> Beh*old yon* simpering *dame*
> Whose face between her forks presages *snow*,
> That minces virtue and does shake the head
> To hear of pleasure's *name* –
> The fitchew *nor* the soilèd *horse* goes to't
> With a *more* riotous *appetite*.

It is almost as though a formal satire in rhymed verse were struggling to escape.

Later, in the speech on the hypocrisy of society and the corruption of the law, the verse becomes regular because it expresses not the aberrations of madness but prophetic insight. It consists, in fact, of variations on the prose speech on the great image of authority, and it looks back to the mock trial of Gonerill and Regan in Act III.

When he recognizes Gloucester, Lear enjoins him to be patient. When he had prayed for patience earlier (II.4.266) it was because of the way he had been treated by Gonerill and Regan; now patience is a virtue that all men need because of the inevitable tragedies of human life. This was a view held not only by pagans: as we have seen, it was shared by many Christian writers, some of whom even thought that the righteous suffer more than others (see p. 44). The idea that we come 'crying hither' was a commonplace – 'to cry and waul presently from the very first hour that he is born into the world'. The idea that we enact our parts on the stage of the world is to be found in many renaissance writers and it was naturally attractive to dramatists. Jaques's speech on the seven ages of man is thought to be an allusion to the motto of the Globe theatre (*Totus mundus agit histrionem*), in which *King Lear* was first performed. The idea was the basis of Calderón's short play entitled *The Grand Theatre of the World*; and Macbeth, after the death of his wife, as the forces of liberation close in on him, compares man with an incompetent actor in a bad melodrama: '... a poor player/That struts and frets his hour upon the stage/And then is heard no more.'

Even closer to the lines in *King Lear* (183–4) is a passage in Sidney's *Arcadia*, a few pages after the source of the Gloucester sub-plot. Plangus, as we have seen (p. 15), as he contemplates suicide, feels – as Gloucester does – that we are the playthings of the gods:

> Like players placed to fill a filthy stage,
> Where change of thoughts one fool to other shows ...
> The child feels that; the man that feeling knows,
> With cries first born, the presage of his life.

Lear's 'stage of fools' is pitying rather than contemptuous, and 'fool' is used throughout the play in a variety of senses. It is a term of endearment, as when Lear calls Cordelia 'my poor fool'. It is a synonym for a court jester, the sage fool whose function is to tell the truth when others conceal it. It is applied to people who are deceived by clever rogues. Shakespeare had read several works by Erasmus, including *Praise of Folly*, in which life is described as 'a kind of comedy, wherein men walk up and down in one another's disguises and act their respective parts, till the property man brings them back to the tiring-house'. Before the end of the book Erasmus moves from satire of the worldly, to show that the unworldly, the holy fools, are the truly wise. He argues that Christianity has a kind of kinship with folly. St Paul in a well-known passage declared that 'God hath chosen the foolish things of the world to confound the wise; and God hath chosen the weak things of the world to confound the things which are mighty'. To the evil characters in the play, the good are foolish.

Cordelia is foolish in refusing to flatter the king; Kent is foolish for taking the part of one who is out of favour; Edgar is foolishly noble and unsuspicious; Albany lacks wisdom and his moral standards are dismissed as foolish moralizing; the Fool is foolish to blurt out inconvenient truths. Yet the worldly-wise – Cornwall, Gonerill, Regan, Edmund, Oswald – prove ultimately to be more foolish than the good people they despise (see p. 38).

[204–285]   After Lear's grotesque flight, Edgar enquires about the forth-coming battle, and the Gentleman replies to the 'peasant' with notable courtesy; another disproof of the riotousness of Lear's followers. Oswald, attempting to kill Gloucester in a situation in which he thinks he has no need of bravery, is himself slain, his last thought being of the delivery of Gonerill's letter (see p. 25). When Edgar reads it he knows that he has damning evidence against Gonerill, and against Edmund.

Scene 7

After his attempt to escape (IV.6.203), Lear has been caught and given a sleeping-draught by the Doctor. It is characteristic of Cordelia that she can eloquently express her love for her father, and her horror at her sisters' treatment of him, before he awakens. The reference to 'Mine enemy's dog' recalls Gloucester's remark about giving shelter to wolves (III.7.62). The lines:

> ... and wast thou fain, poor father
> To hovel thee with swine and rogues forlorn
> In short and musty straw?

do not merely echo *A Mirror for Magistrates* (see p. 13), but they also recall the parable of the Prodigal Son. Lear is the prodigal father, recalled to the forgiving arms of his daughter. When Lear awakens, Cordelia is reduced to taciturnity; but her brief remarks are inexpressibly poignant because we recall her inability in the first scene to tell all her love. She might have been obeying Blake's injunction:

> Never seek to tell thy love,
>   Love that never told must be,
> For the gentle wind doth move
>   Silently, invisibly.

We know that the King of France was right when he defended her reticence, and that it was not a sign of coldness of heart.

The whole of this scene is a supreme example of the use of the simplest words to create the most sublime poetry, made possible by its contrast with the style of previous scenes. Winifred Nowottny was the first to apply Eliot's lines: 'A condition of complete simplicity/(Costing not less than everything)' to the 'lucid stillness' of the style. It may be noted that the percentage of monosyllables is particularly high in the key passage (57–75), about eighty per cent.

Rest, music, and the donning of fresh garments (as in the scene where Pericles is reunited with Marina) are the means by which Lear is restored to sanity; and the precise moment of restoration is marked by the change from 'this lady' to 'my child'. Before this moment Lear imagines that Cordelia is a spirit, 'a soul in bliss', while he is 'bound upon a wheel of fire'. This torture is mentioned in medieval accounts of hell and purgatory, and in the New Testament Apocrypha; it is the punishment inflicted on the damned and it pre-dates Christianity. Shakespeare, remembering that he was writing about a pre-Christian world, blended medieval stories with memories of the punishment of Ixion. This was mentioned by Harsnet, but it would be well known to anyone who had attended a grammar school. It has been suggested that the legend of Ixion was very much in Shakespeare's mind during the writing of the play, especially of Act IV. Centaurs, to whom women are compared by Lear in IV.6, were the adulterous offspring of Ixion, who tried to seduce Juno, and was deceived by a cloud formed in her shape. (The centaurs, however, were male, not female.)

O. B. Hardison argued in a recent article that the Ixion myth provided Shakespeare with 'the philosophical issues in terms of which the action of the play is developed'. Ixion, King of Thessaly, employed a hundred knights, who were called centaurs. This pseudo-historical fact was mythologized to include the frustrated seduction of Juno, and Ixion's subsequent punishment (he was bound to a wheel); and it was allegorized to refer to anyone who, like Lear after the first scene, has only the appearance of rule, without the reality. There were various interpretations of the myth – that it was intended as a warning against the desire for glory; that it was a warning against ingratitude, since Ixion had murdered his father-in-law; or, as Comes put it, through the myth 'the ancients showed that forgetfulness of benefits is the most hateful vice of all to the immortal gods, and it was all the more hateful when a man not only forgets benefits, but even repays them with injuries'. Hardison, from whose article these points are taken, argues that Lear's wish for the pomp of rule without its responsibilities shows that he shares Ixion's illusions; that the storm in Act III parallels the thunderbolt by which Jove cast Ixion into hell; that the theme of ingratitude is exploited throughout the play; and that the myth gave the 'general reasons' which Shakespeare needed to turn the particular facts of the Lear story into a unified drama. (Some of Hardison's points are less convincing than his main argument.)

As we have seen (p. 12), the most memorable scene in the old play of *King Leir* was the one in which Cordella and Leir kneel to each other:

CORDELLA   But look, dear father, look, behold and see
                Thy loving daughter speaketh unto thee. (*She kneels.*)
LEIR   O, stand thou up, it is my part to kneel
                And ask forgiveness for my former faults. (*He kneels.*)
CORDELLA   O, if you wish I should enjoy my breath,
                Dear father, rise, or I receive my death.
LEIR   Then I will rise to satisfy your mind. (*He rises.*)
                But kneel again till pardon be resigned. (*He kneels.*)

The kneeling and rising goes on for another fifty lines. The old dramatist may have realized that the pathos was swamped by absurdity, for he then makes the comic Mumford parody the kneeling. The crude pathos of the scene is condensed and transmuted by Shakespeare into Cordelia's lines:

> O look upon me, sir,
> And hold your hand in benediction o'er me.
> No, sir, you must not kneel.

The incident is recalled in Act V when Lear and Cordelia are led off to prison: 'When thou dost ask me blessing I'll kneel down/And ask of thee forgiveness ...'

The last section of the scene, after the departure of Lear and Cordelia, was cut in the Folio. Although it has been argued that it is dramatically effective to jump from this point to the brutal realism of V.1, the cut is to be deplored. After one of the most moving scenes in all Shakespeare's plays, the audience needs a moment to recover; and the conversation with Kent, on a quieter note, provides the opportunity. It is not *comic* relief, of course, but the rumour that Kent is in Germany lends a touch of irony; and his final remark reminds us how much depends on the forthcoming battle. In a way he may not intend, Kent's own fate is linked with it.

Act V

Scene 1

Edmund, backed by Regan and in command of her forces, has emerged as the equal of Albany in the power-struggle; and, indeed, in his first speech in this scene he sneers at Albany's conscientious scruples and speaks of him with ill-disguised contempt. Hunter assumes that the words 'he's full of alteration/And self-reproving' are addressed to Regan. There is no support for this in either of the early texts; Regan doesn't need to be told what she already knows; and to address the whole speech to a nameless Gentleman would better illustrate Edmund's arrogance. He is, however, in an awkward position with regard to the two sisters. First, he has to swear to Regan, on his honour, that he has not committed adultery with Gonerill; then it is apparent that Gonerill is violently jealous of Regan, who is able, as she is not, to marry Edmund; and he has some slight anxiety because there is no news of Oswald, who was bearing Gonerill's incriminating letter.

In his soliloquy at the end of the scene, Edmund admits that he has sworn love to both sisters, but it is clear that he is interested in them primarily as a means of advancement. He decides, apparently, that if Gonerill murders her husband, he will marry her. What he wants is to be ruler of a united Britain, and that is why he intends to have Lear and Cordelia murdered.

Before this soliloquy, as Albany leaves the stage to attend the council of war, Edgar enters in disguise. He hands Albany the letter written by Gonerill, which he found in Oswald's pocket. The audience, reminded of Oswald's miscarrying a few lines earlier, would know that Albany had received a powerful weapon with which to defeat Gonerill and Edmund. They realize, too, that the mutual hatred of Gonerill and Regan is a destructive force; that Edgar will challenge Edmund, and that he is a more dangerous challenger than he would have seemed a few weeks earlier; and that if Cordelia's forces are defeated, and she and her father are taken prisoner, Edmund intends to have them 'liquidated'. But a happy outcome is still possible, and in Shakespeare's time those members of the audience who were acquainted with the old play may well have expected it.

Scene 2

This brief scene includes the decisive battle in which Cordelia's army is defeated. In the history plays, Shakespeare thought it necessary to show battles on stage. Richmond defeats Richard III, Hal kills Hotspur, and even after *King Lear*, Macduff kills Macbeth on stage. These are all symbolic victories which could not easily be reported. We can see from the apologetic speeches of the Chorus in *Henry V* that Shakespeare was worried by the inadequacy of the means at his disposal – a few ragged foils to represent the battle of Agincourt. In *King Lear* there was no need to present the battle on stage; the results were important, not the skill or courage of the combatants. We hear that Edmund fought well, as we should expect; and we assume that Edgar did too. The battle is therefore covered by a stage-direction of four words between *Exit Edgar* and *Enter Edgar*: *alarum and retreat within* (i.e. off stage).

It will be noted that Edgar's 'Pray that the right may thrive' is ignored by the gods; and that his promise to his father to bring comfort if ever he returns alive is immediately broken by his re-entrance to announce the cold comfort that the right has not thriven. Edgar has also promised Albany that he will return to challenge Edmund, so he could not fight to the death in battle and keep this promise. It could be said, however, that the comfort he intends to give his father is simply a revelation of his identity, rather than the comfort of victory.

The scene is notable for another of Edgar's aphorisms, like many of them a commonplace:

> Men must endure
> Their going hence even as their coming hither;
> Ripeness is all.

It combines Christian beliefs, from the Bible and from the service for the burial of the dead in the Anglican prayer-book, with stoic philosophy which had filtered down into dozens of renaissance books. As Sir Thomas Elyot put it in *The Governor*, a work which Shakespeare is known to have read, '*Maturum* in Latin may be interpreted ripe or ready as fruit when it is ripe, it is at the very point to be gathered and eaten'; and Montaigne has an essay on the theme that 'To philosophize is to learn how to die'. Edgar's words can be paralleled in several of Shakespeare's plays. Hamlet, for example, just before he fights his duel with Laertes, tells Horatio: 'If it be now, 'tis not to come; if it be not to come, it will be now; if it be not now, yet it will come. The readiness is all.' (William Elton devotes a section of his book *King Lear and the Gods* to the prevalence of Edgar's commonplace.)

Scene 3

This long and crowded scene, despite moments when a happy ending seems quite on the cards, leads inexorably to the final catastrophe. As we have suggested, those members of the original audience who remembered the old play, or were acquainted with any of the numerous versions of the Lear story, must have hoped and expected that Lear would be restored to the throne, and that all would be well and 'all manner of thing should be well'.

[1–40] Cordelia's rhymed couplets, like those in the first scene when she says farewell to Gonerill and Regan, remind us of her symbolic significance. They also illustrate her proper pride, her selflessness, and her reliance on proverbial and traditional consolations. Lear, on the other hand, is so overjoyed at being reunited with Cordelia that he welcomes life in prison with her as a kind of paradise. He does not realize, as she apparently does, that their time will be short. He looks forward to an endless repetition of the scene of reunion, and to the acquisition of wisdom through their retirement from the world. They will, he thinks, take upon themselves 'the mystery of things', comprehend the mystery of life and human destiny, which the actual participants, because they are too much involved in the rat-race, cannot understand.

In Hunter's edition, Cordelia's question: 'Shall we not see these daughters and these sisters?' is addressed to Edmund. I feel convinced that, like the rest of the speech, it is addressed to her father. One recent critic has advanced the strange theory that by refusing to see Gonerill and Regan, Lear is virtually committing suicide, and condemning Cordelia to death. In fact, as we learn later, Gonerill has signed the death-warrant; and in view of the former plot on Lear's life it is unlikely that she would be softened by a confrontation with Cordelia. She could never bring herself to plead for mercy and her attitude would be likely to reinforce Gonerill's determination to have her killed.

Lear's second speech is variously interpreted, but it is none the worse for being mysterious. Philip Brockbank has undertaken a detailed discussion of the meaning of the words 'Upon such sacrifices'. What are the sacrifices on which the gods throw incense? Are they the renunciation of the world by Lear and Cordelia? Or are they the sacrifices Cordelia has made for Lear's sake? Or do they denote their mutual forgiveness? Do they look forward to the murder of the innocent victim, Cordelia? Or are they a reference to the familiar text from Psalm 51, 'The sacrifices of God are a contrite spirit'? Do Lear and Cordelia 'assume the mantle of divinity by virtue of their sufferings' (as Apollo does in Keats's *Hyperion*)? Joseph Wittreich includes a picture in *Image of that Horror*, in which an angel of the Apocalypse is casting incense upon the earth in honour of the martyrs.

In the remainder of the speech there seem to be confused echoes of several Old Testament stories: of the destruction of Sodom by a brand from heaven (Genesis 19), of the story of Samson and the foxes (Judges 15), and of Pharaoh's dream of the good and bad years, which was interpreted by Joseph (Genesis 41). The thin ears devour the good ears. Lear appears to mean that he and Cordelia will not weep because they know that Gonerill and Regan will eventually be ruined by their evil prosperity – but other interpretations are possible. Hunter says that 'the tone of the statement seems to be that of a father's homely reassurance to a frightened child'; though he does not imply that the indomitable Cordelia is afraid.

In Kozintsev's film, Edmund gazes at Lear and Cordelia as they are led away, astonished that the defeated and doomed can yet be joyful. This may prepare the way for his belated repentance, but it does not at first alter his ruthless pursuit of power. The Captain who is given the task of executing the prisoners has the opportunity of backing out; but he acquiesces in the crime in words which were inexplicably cut from the Folio text: 'I cannot draw a cart, nor eat dried oats. If it be man's work, I'll do it.' He means: 'I'm not a horse, but a man.' He is afraid of becoming a poor agricultural labourer when he is demobilized. Ironically, his self-serving hastens his own death.

[41–254]   This section of the last scene is on a lower level poetically than the two sections in which Lear himself appears. It has even been suggested that some of the writing is second-rate. Emrys Jones, who afterwards goes on to defend the scene, says that there is 'a whole concentration of by-issues', that it gets 'lost in clogging detail', and that Lear and Cordelia are 'squeezed out' by other characters:

There is in much of it a kind of calculated perfunctoriness or triviality; everyone is frantically, or at least busily (even fussily), self-preoccupied; certainly Shakespeare is withholding something from the writing.

There are several possible answers to these criticisms. First, Shakespeare is tying up the loose ends of the plot, as he was bound to do. Secondly, there are so many exciting things going on that action is for the time being more important than poetic quality. Then the audience, who know that Lear and Cordelia are in peril, although they half forget, still have the knowledge at the back of their minds, so that a feeling of tension is generated. No good play can be on a uniform poetic plateau, and in all Shakespeare's tragedies, either by humorous or by comparatively pedestrian passages, the audience is given a breathing-space before the violent emotional strain of experiencing sublimity. Lastly, if Lear's death-scene, in all its stark simplicity, is to have its full effect, it must be preceded by, and contrasted with, a scene or scenes in a more elaborate, more rhetorical, more 'mannered' style.

Unknown to Edmund, but known to the audience, Gonerill's letter is in Albany's possession. We are waiting to see how the deceived husband will act, but clearly the balance of power is thereby changed. Albany admits that Edmund has fought bravely, but undercuts the admission by adding that he was also lucky. He is naturally concerned for the safety of the royal prisoners, but he has no reason to suspect that as prisoners of war they are in any immediate danger. He does not know that Gonerill and Regan had previously plotted to kill Lear. Edmund, although a general and a duke, is subordinate to the ruler of half Britain. His excuses for imprisoning Lear and Cordelia are plausible: it was a case of protective custody, and sympathy for them might have led to a mutiny of the conscripts. Albany is polite but firm: Edmund is a subordinate, not an equal. This provokes Regan to intervene and to announce that Edmund is her husband, her lord and master; and this in turn leads to Edmund's arrest for high treason, and Albany's challenge, which Edmund accepts. Albany reveals an unexpected sense of black humour in accusing Gonerill:

> 'Tis she is sub-contracted to this lord,
> And I her husband contradict your banns.
> If you will marry, make your loves to me;
> My lady is bespoke.

Regan meanwhile is beginning to feel the effects of Gonerill's poison, whose jealousy is an even stronger motive than her wish to dispose of her husband.

The duel, as critics have pointed out, seems to be medieval in its atmosphere, doubtless under the influence of Sidney's *Arcadia*. The anonymous challenger, the five trumpet calls, the accusation of treason and Edmund's spirited reply remind one of Malory, or of the challenge at the beginning of *Richard II*. The villain is allowed to display courage, which we knew he possessed, but also a noble carelessness, since he could have refused to fight an unknown opponent. Edgar's face is, of course, hidden by his helmet, acquired from the battlefield; but his claim that he is as noble as Edmund, and his knowledge that Edmund had been false to his brother, may well have made Edmund begin to suspect his identity.

Some editors mistakenly give the words 'Save him, save him!' to Gonerill: Albany is anxious that Edmund should not be killed before he has had the opportunity of confessing his crimes, which he does only eleven lines later.

Meanwhile Gonerill's concern for Edmund leads to Albany's production of her letter. He shows her only the signature at the foot of the letter, and hence calls her 'worse than any name'. Defiant to the last, Gonerill claims that she is above the law, that she *is* the law, and cannot be arraigned for her actions. Albany again demands whether she recognizes her letter – some suppose that the question is addressed to Edmund, but as it is Gonerill who replies, this is unlikely. She rushes out to commit suicide, forestalling the attempt to 'govern her' (i.e. control her).

Edmund confesses his misdeeds and, by implication, the yet unacted murder of Lear and Cordelia, which, he says, is 'more, much more'. He forgives his opponent, provided he is of noble birth. In spite of his earlier sneer at legitimacy he could not bear to be killed, as Cornwall had been, by someone of a lower social class. The radical of Act I has become conscious, with his title, of his aristocratic blood. Edgar exchanges forgiveness – even though he has so much more to forgive – and reveals his identity. His comment on the father he loved, the father who has only just died, is regarded by many as harsh, priggish and unloving. It is the main cause of Edgar's unpopularity among critics and readers:

> The gods are just, and of our pleasant vices
> Make instruments to plague us:
> The dark and vicious place where thee he got
> Cost him his eyes.

The main purpose of this statement, Elton argues, was to ease Edmund's last moments 'by offering extenuating comfort in the only terms he is able to comprehend'. The act of adultery in the early months of Gloucester's marriage, an act he remembers with feelings of pleasure, led to the birth of the bastard, the plot to dispossess Edgar, the betrayal of Gloucester and his subsequent blinding. Blinding was, in a sense, an appropriate punishment. Thomas Becon, cited by Elton, claimed that English law was too lenient in dealing with adulterers. 'Among the Locrensians, the adulterers had both their eyes thrust out.' Of course neither Edgar, nor Shakespeare, who had just written *Measure for Measure*, would have agreed with such a savage policy; but Edmund, because the wheel of fortune had come full circle so that he is back where he started, is prepared to accept Edgar's verdict: 'Th'hast spoken right. 'Tis true.'

There follows Edgar's account of his pilgrimage with his father (which softens his remark on the justice of the gods), of the revelation of his identity to his father, and of Gloucester's death, "Twixt two extremes of passion, joy and grief'.

Some critics dislike Edgar so much that they are unable to see the character created by Shakespeare. S. L. Goldberg, in his otherwise sensible book on *King Lear*,[8] describes Edgar as 'the most lethal character in the play'. He kills Oswald, Edmund and Gloucester, and he is the immediate cause of Lear's insanity. This, surely, is absurd. He could not know that the shock would kill his father; by the pretended miracle he had saved him from suicide and despair; and to die in a moment of joy was, one may say, a merciful release. As for his killing of Oswald and Edmund, who would not congratulate him?

Edmund, despite his wickedness and lack of humanity throughout the play, reacts unexpectedly to Edgar's story: 'This speech of yours hath moved me,/And shall perchance do good.' Knowing of the fate which hangs over Lear and Cordelia, the audience expects that Edmund will relent and that this is the 'good' to which he refers. For the next 140 lines, while Edmund remains silent, the tension builds up. Edgar describes his meeting with the dying Kent. (This passage is cut in the Folio text; but if we do not know that Kent is dying – 'The strings of life', Edgar tells us, 'began to crack' – his last entrance and his final meeting with Lear will be ruined.) When the Gentleman arrives with the bloody knife, we may jump to the conclusion that it is Cordelia who has been killed, stabbed as in Holinshed's account.

Albany orders that the bodies of Gonerill and Regan should be brought in. Shakespeare wanted to end the play, as it had begun, with Lear and his three daughters on stage. This time all three are silent. Edmund's comment on seeing the bodies is characteristically egotistical: 'Yet Edmund was beloved.' He had inspired a violent passion in two beautiful, if evil, princesses. Immediately he acts to try to save the lives of Lear and Cordelia, 'some good I mean to do/Despite of mine own nature.'

Several explanations have been offered for his delay in speaking about the sentence of death on Lear and Cordelia. Some critics have blamed Shakespeare for what they regard as the improbable delay, and have concluded that in his determination to have a tragic ending, he did not worry about the improbability. Others argue that although the deaths can no longer advance his career, he had refrained from speaking out of loyalty to Gonerill, who had signed the death-warrant. Once she was dead, his lips were unsealed. This does not quite fit his earlier hint that Edgar's narrative might produce good effects. Another suggestion is that the delay was caused by his slowly activated repentance, set in motion by his realization that he was about to die, and the process completed by the deaths of Gonerill and Regan. His realization that he had been 'beloved', if the violent passions of the sisters could be euphemistically so described, released him from his obsession. The bastard, the deprived child, who had avenged himself on his family and on society (for the pursuit of power, as we have often been told, is a substitute for love), was able at last, but too late, to act morally.

It is Kent, coming to take his final farewell of the king, who reminds Albany that he has forgotten to press Edmund to reveal the whereabouts of his prisoners. Kittredge remarked that the amnesia on everybody's part is just a theatrical necessity to ensure a tragic ending. But 'everybody' is a misnomer. Edgar presumably does not know that Lear and Cordelia have been imprisoned, so that only Albany's forgetfulness is in question. Is it psychologically impossible? Or even improbable? He does not know that the prisoners are in danger, at least in immediate danger; and during the previous quarter of an hour he has had plenty to occupy his mind, or distract his attention: his knowledge of Gonerill's plot against his life, the arrest of Edmund, the illness of Regan, the duel, which he himself will have to fight if the unknown challenger does not turn up, the confrontation with Gonerill, her suicide and the murder of Regan, Edgar's revelation of his identity, his account of his adventures and of the death of Gloucester. In all this crowded schedule there seems to have been no moment when he could reasonably have turned his attention to the question of Lear and Cordelia. The critic who blamed Albany for being more concerned with his marital troubles than with ensuring Lear's safety must have known that he was being unfair. For some obscure reason Albany, like Edgar, attracts snide comments.

Edmund confesses that the official story, to be put out as propaganda, was that Cordelia had hanged herself: 'To lay the blame upon her own despair,/That she fordid herself.' Shakespeare got this idea, as we have seen (p. 11), from the sequel to the Lear story as recounted by Holinshed, Spenser and Higgins, in which Cordelia, years after Lear's death, was deposed by her nephews and imprisoned, so that she killed herself from despair. It is worth noting that Edmund here speaks only of Cordelia: the death of Lear could be ascribed to natural causes.

Albany's prayer for the safety of the captives is immediately followed by the entrance of Lear carrying Cordelia's body. As two recent critics have independently pointed out, the word 'dead' in the stage-direction was added by Rowe, and some doubt on whether she is alive or dead adds to the tension, as Lear's hopes are revived and dashed. The juxtaposition of: 'The gods defend her' and Lear's entrance is bound to be regarded as what Empson called 'a crack at the gods'. In the world of the play prayers are not answered; and Elton believed that Shakespeare was not merely referring to the inefficacy of prayers to pagan gods, which could be taken for granted, but also hinting to the more sophisticated members of the audience that he shared their sceptical attitude to the efficacy of Christian prayers and, indeed, to religion in general (see p. 43). This view is supported by modern agnostics, who assume that the poet was as enlightened as they are themselves. But it may be suggested that the particular religious attitudes embodied in the play are called forth, not by Shakespeare's personal views, but by the setting of the play and by the tragic themes embodied in it. In the tragedies written immediately before and after *King Lear*, Shakespeare goes out of his way to stress that Othello valued the fact that he had been baptized, and his consciousness that he had damned himself, and in *Macbeth* the saintliness of Duncan and Edward the Confessor is contrasted with the sinfulness of the hero and the evil of the weird sisters. In the comedies written in the early years of the seventeenth century Shakespeare paid particular attention to the religious dimension. *Measure for Measure* is the only play with a scriptural title; its heroine is a religious; its central character is disguised as a friar; and its main theme, it has been said, is the problem of how to reconcile the Sermon on the Mount with the exigencies of government. (I see no evidence that Shakespeare in that play was satirizing ideas of providence.) In *All's Well That Ends Well* there is a serious discussion on human depravity and original sin, and even the clown discourses on damnation. It is impossible, therefore, to deduce Shakespeare's personal beliefs from *King Lear* alone; and, if recent textual theories are to be believed, the revision of the play was carried out while he was embarked on the last group of plays (*Cymbeline, Pericles, The Winter's Tale* and *The Tempest*) which are notable for their theophanies.

[255–324] Lear's threefold 'Howl', addressed to all those on stage, seems to reduce mourning to a basic animal cry. Kent's appalled question, 'Is this the promised end?' refers to the end of the world and the Last Judgment. Mary Lascelles suggested[9] that *promised* is an error for *premised*, as in the corresponding passage in *2 Henry VI*, V. As we have seen (p. 50), Shakespeare may have been influenced by pictures of the Last Judgment, showing the separation of the sheep from the goats. The damned are guilty not of flagrant sins – murder, adultery, pride – but of sins of omission, of not looking after the hungry and destitute. Joseph Wittreich's recent book, *Image of that Horror*, uses Kent's question as epigraph and provides a fascinating commentary on the influence of the Apocalypse on the play.

The attempt by the dying Kent to say farewell to his master is frustrated by Lear's concentration on Cordelia and by his failing powers. Kent's reward for his loyal service is to be ranked with the murderers and traitors who interrupt Lear's attempt to resuscitate his daughter. Even when Lear does recognize Kent he is too confused to take in that his servant Caius was the very man. Kent's failure in this scene is another example of 'the heartbreak at the heart of things'.

In the rest of Shakespeare's tragedies the surviving person of highest rank or importance concludes the proceedings, usually with a eulogy of the dead hero – Antony on Brutus, Fortinbras on Hamlet, Lodovico on Othello, Alcibiades on Timon, and Aufidius on his enemy and victim, Coriolanus. Here Albany, following the news of Edmund's death, the last of the villains to die, begins what appears to be the winding-up of the play, resigning his power to Lear, rewarding Edgar and Kent, punishing his enemies. He breaks off in the middle because he notices a change in Lear, a final spurt of energy after his long silence.

'My poor fool' is a term of endearment and it refers to Cordelia, as nearly all editors have recognized. It is important that in this final speech Lear's grief should be focused on Cordelia. Yet Sir Joshua Reynolds confessed that he was one of those who believed that Lear was referring to his Fool. There has been no reference to the Fool since his exit in Act III, and there is no reason to suppose that he, like Cordelia, has been hanged. We have seen that some critics and actors (Brandl, Quiller-Couch, Gielgud) believe that the two roles were played by the same actor. The Fool and Cordelia are never on stage together – the Fool is not present in the first scene, and Cordelia is absent throughout the scenes in which the Fool is present – and it would not have been impossible for the parts to be doubled. It would be interesting to see the experiment tried on the modern stage. Nevertheless, there is a general consensus that the part of the Fool was played by Robert Armin, the first Touchstone, Feste and Lavache. There is no evidence that he ever played women's parts.

Yet the Fool, during Cordelia's absence, continually reminds Lear of his injustice to her, and he acts as a truth-teller in her place. So that those critics who think that Lear in his confused state associates his Fool with the 'poor fool', his daughter, may well be right.

The absolute simplicity of style apparent in the last scene of Act IV is carried a stage further in Lear's dying speech, in which he acknowledges the completeness of his loss:

> No, no, no life!
> Why should a dog, a horse, a rat have life
> And thou no breath at all? Thou'lt come no more;
> Never, never, never, never, never.

All monosyllables, except for the tolling of the five-fold 'Never'. Out of context these lines would be prosaic, and the next line could be regarded as flat and feeble – 'Pray you undo this button. Thank you, sir.' Yet in context they are supreme examples of dramatic poetry. But their effectiveness depends on the way in which they contrast with the more elaborate style of previous scenes. It is important not to fall into the error of those critics who contrast the artificiality of rhetoric with the sincerity of simplicity. In reading some critics, one has the feeling that they would have preferred a Shakespeare who wrote in prose.

The critics are divided on the question of the button – whether it was Cordelia's or Lear's. Those who believe it was Cordelia's argue that when she is carried in by Lear, she is not certainly dead, that the prevailing method of execution by hanging involved strangulation, that the execution had been interrupted by Lear when he killed the executioner, that he was not foolish in trying to revive her, and that the undoing of the button was a sensible means to this end. Those, on the other hand, who believe that the button was Lear's, point to the fact that in the storm he had tried to unbutton his garments, so that he could be identified with unaccommo-dated man. Now he wants to shake off what Shakespeare elsewhere calls 'this muddy vesture of decay'. From the physiological point of view, Lear is suffering from the feeling of suffocation, the *hysterica passio*, the mounting sorrow of which he had spoken earlier.

At the very end Lear thinks he sees a movement of Cordelia's lips (air released by the unbuttoning?) and Bradley declared that Lear died of joy in the belief that she was, after all, alive – a chance that would redeem all sorrows that ever he had felt. Opponents of Bradley have argued that such an interpretation sentimentalized the utter bleakness of the ending. Yet it would appear to be the most natural interpretation of the line. It is supported by the close parallel with the death of Gloucester, whose heart 'burst smilingly', and this in turn was based on the death of the Paphlagonian king (see p. 109), whose broken heart is given its *coup de grâce* by excess of comfort. Why critics should imagine that Bradley's interpretation *softens* the tragedy is strange indeed; for the audience knows that Lear is deluded, and surely this intensifies the horror of the ending:

it is the last twist of the knife. (A few theologically-minded critics have argued that Lear's last words are a foretaste or symbol of the Resurrection, but it is difficult to believe that Shakespeare meant us to understand the words in this sense.)

Kent's reference to 'the rack of this tough world' is the final example in the play of the iterative image, isolated and analysed by Caroline Spurgeon, of a tortured human body (see p. 39). It is an image that goes beyond the sufferings of Lear, or indeed of any one character in the play. It refers ultimately to everyman and to the inescapable tragedy of humanity, 'struggling in vain with ruthless destiny', as Wordsworth put it, and 'born under one law, to another bound', as Shakespeare's contemporary Fulke Greville said. 'Longer' is a quibble: it means for a longer time, and also for the body to be stretched out further on the rack, with increasing agony.

Albany's abdication in favour of Lear is overtaken by events. At the end he begs Kent and Edgar to be joint rulers, as Lear had abdicated in favour of Albany and Cornwall. Kent refuses because he knows that he will shortly follow his master. Edgar, in the last speech of the play, tacitly accepts the responsibility. (It may be mentioned that this speech is given to Albany in the Quarto, either by mistake, or because Shakespeare changed his mind.) Edgar in his time has played many parts, and his final role is that of king. F. T. Flahiff has pointed out that the historical King Edgar is mentioned by Elyot as one in whose reign the realm was united, reason revived, 'and the land began to take comfort and to show some visage of the public weal'. This was, in fact, long after Lear's time; but that Edgar was Lear's godson – an anachronism that takes him out of the pagan world of the play – made it appropriate for him to succeed his godfather, especially as the other, historical, Edgar restored order and stability to a divided kingdom. The Edgar of the play would sustain the gored state. But if the new era was to be freed from the horrors of the old, Edgar knew that his generation would not rival the old in its extremity of suffering and would be without the sacrifices on which the gods throw incense.

Appendix

The Text

Modern editions of *King Lear* are all based on two early texts which differ considerably from each other. These are the First Quarto (Q1), published in 1608, and the version published in 1623, seven years after Shakespeare's death, in the collection of thirty-six of his plays known as the First Folio (F1). In between these two editions was another quarto (Q2), published in 1619, but misleadingly dated 1608. This was a reprint of Q1, with some emendations and some additional misprints. F1 was printed from Q1 (and possibly from a few pages of Q2), but heavily corrected so as to bring it into line with the prompt-book. (This, however, is disputed: some scholars think it was based directly on a manuscript, and it has even been argued that this manuscript was the same as that used for Q1, after it had been tidied up.)

The text of Q1 is longer by some 300 lines than that of F1, though F1 contains a few lines not in Q1, notably the Fool's prophecy in III.2. Where the texts can be compared, F1 is greatly superior. It has been estimated that a third of the verse lines in Q1 are divided incorrectly, and that 500 lines of verse are mistakenly printed as prose. The mistakes may be due to the difficulty in deciphering the manuscript, or to careless printers; and the failure to recognize verse was doubtless due to Shakespeare's habit of writing verse lines without initial capitals.

The nature of the manuscript is a matter of controversy. It is argued by some that it was in Shakespeare's own handwriting, or a copy of it; at the other extreme, it is argued that the text is so bad that it must have been compiled from memory, by one, or two, or the whole company of actors, when they needed a temporary prompt-book while on tour in the provinces. In any case, it is generally agreed that F1 provides a more reliable text, and that it often corrects the mistakes of Q1, occasionally adding some of its own. Sometimes the editors of the Folio tried to improve on Shakespeare, eliminating obscurities and correcting his grammar, and it is suspected that words substituted by actors got into the prompt-book and hence into the Folio text.

The main problem confronting a modern editor who decides to base his text on F1 is what to do about the 300 lines omitted from it. Till the last few years, all modern editors (Duthie, Muir, Dover Wilson, Hunter), not wishing to lose any lines written by the greatest of English poets, have inserted the lines from Q1. But recently a number of scholars, English and American, have argued that such a composite text is a monstrosity, representing neither the play as it was first performed, nor the revised version preserved in F1; that there were two distinct acting versions; that Shakespeare himself was responsible for the cuts, and that we ought to respect his wishes.[1]

Against this, it has been pointed out that it is not certain that the cuts were Shakespeare's and that, even if they were, they may have been made reluctantly for a particular purpose – for example a reduced cast, a provincial tour, a different stage, or the need to shorten the length of the performance of what was one of Shakespeare's longest plays. (When I directed the play, I was forced to cut half-an-hour from it to enable members of the audience to catch the last buses.) If the circumstances changed, the cut passages might well have been restored. It is true that most of the revisions (as opposed to the cuts) are obvious improvements. Some of them, one suspects, restore what Shakespeare wrote but which the Q1 printers garbled.

Several critics have defended every one of the cuts, arguing that by them the play has been greatly improved, as well as shortened. This view is one I find completely untenable.[2] Some of the cuts are discussed in the Commentary, above; and Hunter's edition provides the evidence on which the reader can decide for himself.

The play is very long and it would be impossible, even with the Folio cuts and with the more rapid delivery of Shakespeare's own company, to perform it in what he called 'the two hours traffic of the stage'. But this phrase was spoken early in his career, and many of the later tragedies – *Hamlet*, *Othello* and *Antony and Cleopatra* – are as long as, or longer than, *King Lear*.

Two other textual matters should be mentioned. Quartos of plays were printed hurriedly and as cheaply as possible. Proof-correction was carried out after the actual printing had begun. The uncorrected sheets were not thrown away, as they should have been, but bound up with the corrected sheets. This means that in the twelve extant copies of *King Lear* (Q1) there are 167 variants (differences between different copies). Each of these twelve copies had different combinations of corrected and uncorrected sheets. We can easily ascertain which of the variants were corrections and which were not. Hunter gives examples on pp. 324–6 of his New Penguin Shakespeare edition: e.g. II.1.119, III.4.12, IV.2.29, IV.2.60, V.3.48. It would be nice to think that the corrections were always right. Unfortunately a few of the uncorrected readings, though wrong, may be closer to what Shakespeare wrote than the corrected readings, which may be merely guesses, or represent another attempt to decipher a difficult manuscript. One example of the problems involved is given in the Commentary, above, on IV.1.10.

The other matter is equally tricky. If the Folio text, in spite of its many alterations, was derived directly or indirectly from the Q1 text, some of the necessary changes would doubtless have been overlooked. This means that the Folio text is generally more reliable where it differs from Q1 than when it agrees with it.

All editors introduce scores of readings which are neither in Q1 nor in F1. Many of these were first introduced by one or other of the eighteenth- or nineteenth-century editors. Although in recent years some of the readings of Q1 and F1 have been restored, and editors are now more reluctant to emend, the process still continues.

There are bound to be differences of opinion between editors. Hunter, for example, lists more than a hundred readings in which he differs from other modern editors; but the differences hardly affect our interpretation of the play as a whole. An edition which followed Q1 and ignored all F1 improvements, or one which followed F1 and omitted the lines peculiar to Q1, would alter marginally our assessment of Albany and Edgar, but there would be no radical change in our understanding of the meaning of the play.

Date

King Lear was written after March 1603 and before Boxing Day 1606. These limits are determined by precise facts. One of the books which was frequently echoed in the play was a topical pamphlet by Samuel Harsnet, *A Declaration of Egregious Popishe Impostures* (see p. 15). This was registered for publication in March 1603, and unless Shakespeare read it in manuscript, for which there is no evidence and no likelihood, the play must have been written after that date.

When the play was published in 1608, it was stated on the title-page that it had been performed before the king at Whitehall on St Stephen's night, that is, 26 December. This was not 1607, however, because when the play was registered in November 1607, reference was made to the royal performance, so that this must have been in 1606. But as plays were often tried out at the Globe before they were performed at court, *King Lear* may have been given an earlier performance.

Many attempts have been made to narrow down the date of composition, but with conflicting results, as the following summary shows.

(1) It has been argued that Gloucester's reference to 'These late eclipses in the sun and moon' (I.2.103) was an allusion to the eclipses of September and October 1605. It has been suggested, too, that there is some resemblance between Gloucester's words and a pamphlet published in February 1606, which speaks of

> traytrous Designements, Catching at Kingdomes, translation of Empyre, downefall of menn in Authoritye, aemulations, Ambition, Innovations, Factious Sects, Schisms, and much disturbance and trobles in religion and matters of the Church, with many other thinges infallible in sequent such orbicall positions and Phaenomenes.

The resemblance appears to be slight, and astrological jargon does not greatly vary from age to age, so there is no need to suppose that the play was written after February 1606. There had been eclipses in 1601, and Shakespeare could have been referring to these, to those of 1605, or to no particular eclipses. If he was alluding to those of 1605, the play must have been written after October 1605 – unless he cunningly referred to them in advance.

(2) The source-play, *King Leir*, to which Shakespeare was greatly indebted (see p. 11), was registered in May 1605 and published after that date. According to the title-page, this play had been 'divers and sundry times lately acted'. But it has been argued that such an old play, written in 1590 or earlier, is not likely to have been revived in the seventeenth century, and that the publisher hoped that people would purchase *King Leir* in the belief that it was Shakespeare's play. This theory is supported by the curious fact that in the Stationers' Register the words *Tragecall historie* replaced *Tragedie*: this would suggest that the clerk made the mistake because Shakespeare's play had already been performed. It is worth noting that *King Leir* had been registered originally in 1594 but had not been published for eleven years, and a publisher may have thought it worth while to publish it in 1605 because of the success of Shakespeare's play. On the other hand, it is pointed out that some plays as old as *King Leir* were revived with great success in the seventeenth century. We are therefore left with conflicting theories: that Shakespeare wrote his play soon after the publication of *King Leir*; or that his play had been performed before May 1605 – in which case Shakespeare must have relied on memories of the old play, or possibly on a manuscript, rather than on the printed text.

(3) Shakespeare had acted in Jonson's *Sejanus* in 1603 and he echoed

some lines from the first scene (23–38) in Kent's abuse of Oswald (II.2.70ff.).*Sejanus* was not published until 1605 and it has been argued that a prefatory poem by William Strachey contains echoes of the storm-scenes of *King Lear*. If the resemblances were not accidental, as I suspect, the storm-scenes must have been written some months before August 1605.

(4) It has been argued by Gary Taylor that Shakespeare was influenced by *Eastward Hoe*, a comedy written by Jonson, Chapman and Marston, performed in 1605, and published after 4 September in the same year. Taylor argued, therefore, that *King Lear* could not have been written before the autumn of 1605. But the resemblance between the two plays, slight as they are, would not have required knowledge of the published text. They could just as easily have been derived from a performance. Shakespeare would certainly have been to see it. He could therefore have written the relevant scenes any time after the spring of 1605.

(5) Brian Annesley, a gentleman pensioner of Queen Elizabeth, died insane on 10 July 1604. His eldest daughter, Lady Wildgosse, together with her husband, contested his will. The youngest daughter, who had looked after her father during his last years, appealed to Cecil; and in December 1604 the Prerogative Court upheld the will which favoured the loving daughter. As Shakespeare was often at court, as Groom of the Chamber and as supplier of plays and performer, he may well have heard of this dispute and been impressed by the coincidence that the loving daughter was named Cordell. Another coincidence is that Cordell after-wards married William Harvey, who had been the third husband of the dowager Countess of Southampton, the mother of Shakespeare's patron; and Harvey is thought by some to be the mysterious 'Mr W. H.' who is thanked by the publisher of Shakespeare's *Sonnets*. Lear does not go mad in any version of the story before Shakespeare's, and if this idea was suggested by the story of Annesley and his three daughters, we could deduce that the play was written after July 1604.

(6) Another line of argument concerns possible links with the court performance on St Stephen's night. Joseph Wittreich has called attention to some echoes in the play of passages appointed to be read in church on that day.[3] This might suggest either that the 1606 performance was the first, or that Shakespeare knew that it was going to take place. In which case *King Lear* was written as late as 1606.

(7) There are a number of close links between *King Lear* and other plays of Shakespeare, notably *Othello*, *Measure for Measure* and *Timon of Athens*; and the links with these plays seem to be more substantial than those with *Macbeth*. As Bradley pointed out, *Othello* and *King Lear*

contain words Shakespeare does not use elsewhere (for example, *waterish*, *potential*, *unbonnetted* and *deficient*), some words used in a sense peculiar to the two plays, and a number of phrases (for example, *fortune's alms*, *stand in hard/bold/cure, perforce/needs/must wither*). Justice and authority are debated in *King Lear* and *Measure for Measure*, and there are several words Shakespeare used only in *All's Well That Ends Well*, *Troilus and Cressida* and these two plays. The theme of ingratitude dominates *King Lear* and *Timon of Athens*, and there are several verbal parallels. It is reasonable to suppose that these six plays belong to the same period of Shakespeare's career; but as there is no general agreement about the dates of these plays, they do not help us to give an exact date for the composition of *King Lear*. It should be remembered, too, that similarity of subject-matter can call up vocabulary associated with it. It has often been pointed out that *Macbeth* echoes *Lucrece*, written at least a dozen years earlier; and the mad-scenes of *King Lear* echo the mad-scenes of *Titus Andronicus*, written at the very beginning of Shakespeare's career, fifteen or even twenty years previously. Echoes do not necessarily mean proximity of date.

It will be seen that these seven methods of establishing a more accurate date, each one plausible when considered in isolation, are completely contradictory when considered together. We are driven to conclude that the play was written between March 1603 and December 1606, and probably in the second half of that period. Even this is open to an objection. *Macbeth* was begun after the visit of James I to Oxford, where he saw a playlet about the prophecy of his reputed ancestor, Banquo, that his descendants would rule for ever. There are allusions to the execution of Father Garnet for complicity in the Gunpowder Plot, and to the hanging of traitors, passages which may be interpolations but must have been written in the spring or summer of 1606. If, therefore, *King Lear* was being written in 1605–6, its composition would have overlapped with that of *Macbeth*. Although *King Lear* could be dated rather later, this would go against the conviction of many critics that *Macbeth* was the later play.

Notes

Anyone who writes on *King Lear* is bound to be indebted to scores of previous critics. The purpose of these notes is to acknowledge the more obvious of these debts, and also to enable students to follow up lines of enquiry if they feel so disposed.

Three anthologies of criticism may be mentioned:

Aspects of 'King Lear', ed. Kenneth Muir and Stanley Wells (Cambridge University Press, 1982)

King Lear: A Casebook, ed. Frank Kermode (Macmillan, 1969)

King Lear: Critical Essays, ed. Kenneth Muir (Garland, 1984).

INTRODUCTION

1. Lamb's essay, 'On the Tragedies of Shakespeare' (1811), is often reprinted; Harley Granville-Barker's reply is in his *Prefaces to Shakespeare*, First Series (1927).

2. The two films of *King Lear* are interestingly contrasted. Peter Brook's, with Paul Schofield in the title role, assumes that life is meaningless or absurd. Gregori Kozintsev's film, using Pasternak's translation, interprets the play as an attack on injustice. Of the two television versions, the BBC one is worthy but uninspired; the ITV version has the advantage of a great performance by Laurence Olivier.

3. A. C. Bradley, *Shakespearean Tragedy* (1904).

THE MAKING OF THE PLAY

1. See the article by Barbara Heliodora Carneiro de Mendonça in *Shakespeare Survey* 13 (1960).

2. *As You Like It*, II.7.175; *Julius Caesar*, III.2.185; *Twelfth Night*, III.4.338.

3. See Geoffrey Bullough, *Narrative and Dramatic Sources of Shakespeare* (1973), and Kenneth Muir, *The Sources of Shakespeare's Plays* (1977).

4. These are summarized in the New Arden edition of the play.

5. See, for example, IV.6.183–4.

6. Fitzroy Pyle in *Modern Language Review* (1948), pp. 449–55.

7. A. C. Bradley, *Shakespearean Tragedy* (1904).

CHARACTERIZATION

1. Kenneth Muir, *Shakespeare Contrasts and Controversies* (1985), p. 9.

2. Leo Kirschbaum, *Character and Characterization in Shakespeare* (1962).

3. S. L. Goldberg, *An Essay on 'King Lear'* (1974).

THEMES AND IMAGES

1. Robert Heilman, *This Great Stage* (1948), pp. 41ff.
2. J. I. M. Stewart, *Character and Motive in Shakespeare* (1949), p. 23
3. W. R. Elton, *King Lear and the Gods* (1966), p. 111.
4. This is the last stanza of 'William Bond':

> Seek Love in the Pity of others' Woe,
> In the gentle relief of another's care,
> In the darkness of night and the winter's snow,
> In the naked and outcast, seek Love there!

5. Enid Welsford, *The Fool* (1961), p. 271.
6. Richard G. Moulton, *Shakespeare as a Dramatic Artist* (1892), p. 217.
7. Section entitled 'The Animal in Man' in *This Great Stage*, op. cit.
8. G. Wilson Knight, *The Wheel of Fire* (1930).
9. W. H. Clemen, *The Development of Shakespeare's Imagery* (1951), pp. 133 53.
10. A. C. Bradley, *Shakespearean Tragedy* (1904).
11. *Some Facets of 'King Lear'*, ed. Colie and Flahiff (1974), chapter 5.
12. Caroline Spurgeon, *Shakespeare's Imagery* (1935), p. 339.
13. W. H. Gardner, *Gerard Manley Hopkins* (1944), I.175.
14. John Danby, *Elizabethan and Jacobean Poets* (1965), pp. 108ff.
15. Curtis Brown Watson, *Shakespeare and the Renaissance Concept of Honor* (1960), p. 318.
16. Joseph Wittreich, *Image of that Horror* (1984), p. 105.
17. Elton, op. cit., chapter 1.
18. Robert Speaight, *Nature in Shakespearian Tragedy* (1955), p. 121.
19. Elton, op. cit., p. 338.
20. Lucien Goldmann, *The Hidden God* (1964).
21. George Gordon, *Shakespearian Comedy* (1944), pp. 126–8.
22. Ovid, *Metamorphoses*, trans. A. Golding (1567), XV.74ff.
23. Robert Ornstein, *The Moral Vision of Jacobean Tragedy* (1960).
24. Maynard Mack, *King Lear in Our Time* (1965).
25. Kott, I understand, no longer holds these views.
26. Susan Snyder, *The Comic Matrix of Shakespeare's Tragedies* (1979), p. 140.
27. In *Some Facets of 'King Lear'*, op. cit. Colie's chapter, mentioned in the next paragraph, is in the same book, pp. 185ff.
28. John Danby, *Shakespeare's Doctrine of Nature* (1949), pp. 20ff.
29. G. Kozintsev, *King Lear: The Space of Tragedy* (1977), p. 251.
30. Mary Lascelles, in *Shakespeare Survey* 26 (1973).
31. Wittreich, op. cit.
32. Introduction to his edition.
33. John Holloway, *The Story of the Night* (1961).
34. L. C. Knights, *Some Shakespearean Themes* (1959), p. 119.

COMMENTARY
1. See Brian Vickers's article in *Modern Language Review* (1968), pp. 305ff.
2. Leo Kirschbaum, *Character and Characterization in Shakespeare* (1962).
3. Emrys Jones, *Scenic Form in Shakespeare* (1971).
4. Gary Taylor, 'The War in *King Lear*', in *Shakespeare Survey* 33 (1980).
5. Kenneth Muir, 'Madness in *King Lear*', in *Shakespeare Survey* 13 (1960)
6. Edmund Blunden, *Shakespeare's Significances* (1929).
7. Walter Raleigh, *Shakespeare* (1907).
8. S. L. Goldberg, *An Essay on 'King Lear'* (1974).
9. Mary Lascelles, '*King Lear* and Doomsday', in *Shakespeare Survey* 26 (1973).

APPENDIX
1. Apart from numerous articles, there are two important books on the text; one by Steven Urkowitz, *Shakespeare's Revision of 'King Lear'* (1980), and the other a collection of essays edited by Gary Taylor and Michael Warren, entitled *The Division of the Kingdoms* (1983).
2 See Kenneth Muir, *Shakespeare Contrasts and Controversies* (1985)
3 Joseph Wittreich, *Image of that Horror* (1984), p. 116.

FOR THE BEST IN PAPERBACKS, LOOK FOR THE

In every corner of the world, on every subject under the sun, Penguin represents quality and variety – the very best in publishing today.

For complete information about books available from Penguin – including Pelicans, Puffins, Peregrines and Penguin Classics – and how to order them, write to us at the appropriate address below. Please note that for copyright reasons the selection of books varies from country to country.

In the United Kingdom: For a complete list of books available from Penguin in the U.K., please write to *Dept E.P., Penguin Books Ltd, Harmondsworth, Middlesex, UB7 0DA*

In the United States: For a complete list of books available from Penguin in the U.S., please write to *Dept BA, Penguin, 299 Murray Hill Parkway, East Rutherford, New Jersey 07073*

In Canada: For a complete list of books available from Penguin in Canada, please write to *Penguin Books Canada Ltd, 2801 John Street, Markham, Ontario L3R 1B4*

In Australia: For a complete list of books available from Penguin in Australia, please write to the *Marketing Department, Penguin Books Australia Ltd, P.O. Box 257, Ringwood, Victoria 3134*

In New Zealand: For a complete list of books available from Penguin in New Zealand, please write to the *Marketing Department, Penguin Books (NZ) Ltd, Private Bag, Takapuna, Auckland 9*

In India: For a complete list of books available from Penguin, please write to *Penguin Overseas Ltd, 706 Eros Apartments, 56 Nehru Place, New Delhi, 110019*

In Holland: For a complete list of books available from Penguin in Holland, please write to *Penguin Books Nederland B.V., Postbus 195, NL–1380AD Weesp, Netherlands*

In Germany: For a complete list of books available from Penguin, please write to *Penguin Books Ltd, Friedrichstrasse 10 – 12, D–6000 Frankfurt Main 1, Federal Republic of Germany*

In Spain: For a complete list of books available from Penguin in Spain, please write to *Longman Penguin España, Calle San Nicolas 15, E–28013 Madrid, Spain*